Finding the Work You Love

A Woman's Career Guide

ASTRID BERG, M.S.

D1247232

Resource Publications, Inc.
San Jose, California

Other Books by Astrid Berg

Career Metamorphosis
Creatavision

Editorial director: Kenneth Guentert
Managing editor: Elizabeth J. Asborno
Cover design and illustrations: Terri Ysseldyke-All

Reprint Department
Resource Publications, Inc.
160 E. Virginia Street #290
San Jose, CA 95112-5876

Library of Congress Cataloging-in-Publication Data
Berg, Astrid, 1955-
    Finding the work you love : a woman's career guide / Astrid Berg.
        p.   cm.
    Includes bibliographical references.
    ISBN 0-89390-269-1
    1. Vocational guidance for women—United States. 2. Women—United States—Employment. I. Title.
    HF5382.65.B46   1993
    331.7'02'082—dc 20   93-28936

Printed in the United States of America.

98 97 96 95 94 | 5 4 3 2 1

CONTENTS

      Women Have Their Own Process
      ExpressYourself
      Profiles and Exercises

      Profiles: *Paula, Maureen, Maria, and Sara*

Part One: Background

      How It Was: Women in the Home
      How It Is: Women in the Home and Workplace
      How It Could Be: Success and Balance

Part Two: Self-Assessment

Part Three: Taking Action

TABLES

ACKNOWLEDGMENTS

To the many women I have encountered over the years who have inspired me with their lives, courage and visions. In particular, I wish to thank Anne Berg, Johanna Berg, Lauralyn Bauer, Jaime Beisley, Laura Belson, Linda Brown, Patty Casci, Liz Cass, Maureen Cleary, Lisa Coplantz, Dawn Corcoran, Alice Corkery, Mildred Couwenberg, Els Drievoet, Barrie Egen-Auld, Kelly Ferry, Mary Ferry, Michelle Ferry, Susan Ferry, Ginny Fletcher, Charlotte Franken, Judith Grutter, Joyce Hahn, Joyce Harijono, Tracy Hart, Karen Hecht, Sharon Hoffman, Anna Kastelein, Camille Kulka, Kathy Looman, Chris McLain, Patty McLoon, Sheree McPeak, Kathy Middleton, Carolyn Motokane, Solvie Mount, Cindy Nelis, Donna Nelis, Mary O'Connell, Miriam Pitts, Crystal Poe, Virginia Poe, Dean Porter, Peggie Powers, Inge Rhemrev, Connie Rose, Mary Seebart, Johanna Sharp, Gery Shayne, Marsha Sinetar, Ellen Skaggs, Marky Stein, Olga Stone, Judy Strothers, Cynthia Tidball, Irene van den Kolk, Suzanne van Eden, Anne Wallace, and Joanne Zeldenrust.

How This Guide Will Help You Find the Work You Love

Ideas for this book began to formulate as I was counseling women who were entering or re-entering the workforce or who were changing careers. I realized that the use of standard tools, theories and resources for career counseling did not always apply to the female gender. Based on my experiences working with women, I have adapted male-oriented theories to relate more closely to the psychology of women and have included pertinent women's issues such as childcare and balancing home and career, which are not normally addressed in career planning books.

Women Have Their Own Process

SINCE WORLD WAR II, WOMEN HAVE entered the world of work in increasing numbers. Birth control and the women's movement have created new opportunities for women to become and do more than our mothers would have even dared

1

to dream. Yet, the women's movement is not old enough to provide role models, and socialization often teaches the ideologies of our mothers' and grandmothers' time. We are confused about our roles and have conflicting desires. Although we want careers, financial independence and recognition as leaders, we also want to have families, to feel feminine and to experience life balance. How do we combine all these wants? And can we *truly* have everything?

Express Yourself

BY EXPRESSING NEEDS OF OUR TRUE selves, women may look forward to a progressive future. Look within yourself for the answer. Your solution may be different from that of your dearest friend. More importantly, recognize that you have a choice. Existentialists believe that free choice creates anxiety. With a lack of choice, you have less anxiety but also less opportunity. In seeking to understand, you can unfold and discover a dream or purpose you may never have realized you possessed. In your effort to discover your personal answer, you will uncover what is appropriate for you, whether it is to become or remain a homemaker, or whether you choose to be a self-made millionaire before you are thirty.

My purpose is to help you realize your career and your life aspirations. This book is designed as a step-by-step process to aid in identifying who you are, in exploring the world of work, and in fulfilling your career, family and personal needs with balance. Each chapter addresses a specific area of exploration and provides exercises to help you gain insight to those topics of inquiry. In each chapter, you will find profiles of four women who have completed the recommended exercises.

In the first stage of the process, you will uncover your history, personality traits, interests, skills and values, and you will learn to understand how they relate to career and lifestyle alternatives. Knowing which personality traits you express and suppress and how you would like to manifest yourself at work and in your personal life is a key to life fulfillment. You will identify interests from different realms and stages in your life and cluster them into patterns. You will discover skills and talents from work and commonplace activities, and you will learn how to translate these into marketable skills.

In the second stage, you will integrate these five aspects of yourself and explore career/life options. You will uncover your career/life goal through inner and outer exploration, which, in the end, will lead to a bringing together of your fantasies and what you can actualize in reality.

Profiles and Exercises

FOLLOWING IS AN INTRODUCTION TO four women who are experiencing their own career transitions. They represent different needs, personalities and backgrounds, and their stories will facilitate your understanding of the career development process. In their completion of the exercises, the characters illustrate what is necessary to arrive at a balance between career and personal aspirations. As you read each chapter, choose among and complete the exercises that motivate and facilitate your own process.

To use the guided visualizations in this book, try one of these options:

1. Read the visualization onto a cassette tape beforehand, or

2. Work with a friend, taking turns reading the visualizations to each other.

Whichever option you choose, it is important to read the visualizations slowly, including pauses.

Profile: Paula Dombrowski

She stood staring into the mirror, her mind racing over the years: Kelly's first ballet recital, hunching over the kitchen table to help Tom with his homework, little Susan graduating from high school, and faces of children rushing in and out of the house. Now there was only silence and emptiness.

The sound of the car pulling into their driveway brought Paula back to the present. Her thoughts possessed her as she finished dressing for the evening. Who do I think I am going to class with all those young college kids? I'll feel out of place.

"Who are you trying to impress, the teacher or the students?" Her husband interrupted her thoughts.

"Is this too much?" Paula returned. Her slacks and sweater were simple but stylish.

"You look fine. Better hurry, traffic is bad." He pecked her on the cheek, and turned to go down stairs.

Knowing she didn't have time, Paula went ahead and changed into a pair of jeans and sneakers and kept on the oversized sweater. She rushed downstairs to find Jim reading the paper.

"I left your dinner in the oven. I should be back by nine."

"Make sure you don't walk to your car alone," Jim returned.

Paula left to attend a class that she hoped would tell her what to do with the rest of her life.

Profile: Maureen Casey

Ear to the phone and nodding her head, Maureen checked her watch. With her free hand, she organized the papers on her desk. If this client went on for much longer, she'd be late. Maybe it wasn't a good idea to take a class right now. How many times would she be pressed to get there on time?

"I'll recheck all of the arrangements myself and get back to you in the morning, Ms. Cass."

Pause.

"Bye."

Click. She finished straightening her desk, jotted some notes on her calendar, and reached in her drawer for her pocketbook. She took the Liz Claiborne suit jacket that hung behind her office door and slipped it on. There wasn't time to stop in the ladies room. Glancing at her watch, she rushed out the door and down the hall.

"Where are you off to?" It was Eva, the company gossip.

"I have an art class," she lied.

"Art?" Eva was puzzled.

Maureen waved in response, entered the elevator and pushed "Garage." She hoped that no one would find out that she was taking a what-do-I-want-to-do-when-I-grow-up class. Instead, there will be questions about art. Oh dear...

Profile: Maria Diego

"Remember, you'll be staying overnight with Tia Elena." said Maria while strapping her son into the car seat.

"For the whole night?" the four-year-old questioned tentatively.

"Uh-huh," she answered before walking around to her side of the car.

"Will you be there?"

"No, but your sister will when she comes home from school."

"Where will you sleep?" his questions continued.

"At home, but I won't be home for dinner because I'm going to school."

"When can I go to school, Mama?"

"Soon enough, Joey." While starting her engine, Maria's mind drifted back to her senior year, so anxious to get out, so excited about the future. She was to marry that summer. So much had happened since then. If she had only known...

Profile: Sara Harris

Haphazardly stacked papers and books and several empty tea mugs sat on the heavy oak dining table. Leaning over a book, Sara noticed that the light was getting dim. A vague feeling of urgency came over her. She got up to check her calendar and peered at the clock on her mantel. It read 5:40. No time for dinner. She was dressed in sweats and her black curls were carelessly pinned up on top of her head. Opening the refrigerator, she thought, How many days have passed since I've been to the store? I get too absorbed in my papers. She grabbed the last Granny Smith, promising to take better care of herself. She left eager with anticipation of tonight's class. Pulling out of the driveway, she noticed the Empty sign on the fuel gauge and decided that her Honda could make the ten-mile drive to the community college.

Part One

Background

CHAPTER I

Changing World,
Changing Work,
Changing Women

How It Was:
Women in
the Home

AMERICA BEGAN AS A NATION OF FAMILY farmers wherein men, women and children worked together at or near the home, and work related to family subsistence. Women's duties included cooking, baking, spinning, weaving, sewing, farming, and caring for and butchering animals. The making of goods and tools used for daily work activities was also women's work. Lack of time made housecleaning efforts negligible. Young children were kept close, and older children helped both parents. The advent of the industrial revolution coaxed men, and some women, to a place of work outside the home. As more men left home to go to work, the sexes became segregated and two diverse worksettings developed. At the same time, men and women were separated within the workplace, and the stereotypes of women's work and men's work became resolute. In addition to the segregation of work between the sexes, hierarchy in industry developed.[1] At home, women pursued household and childcare duties, but items formerly made at home were purchased; thus, it became essential to earn money. To make extra income, women took in sewing, laundry, or boarders, while some went into the factories to work.

During the ensuing hundred years, many women joined the men and left home to work. In the late nineteenth century, less than twenty-five percent of women worked outside of the home. Those who did were either unmarried or were mothers not receiving support from their husbands.

During World War II, America needed women to fill jobs normally held by men and to help with the war effort. The female gender participated in skilled labor and had responsibilities that were later given back to returning war veterans.

Women's participation in the workforce decreased in the fifties concurrently with the baby boom and the move to the suburbs. In a growing economy, the post-war years freed married women from earning money to devote to homemaking and childcare. As a result, clothes and homes became cleaner, and meals were more intricate and exotic. Modern appliances and conveniences, designed to simplify housekeeping, raised homemakers' standards and actually increased the time they spent on chores. During these years, married women were not hired, and being a full-time housewife was considered a privileged position.[2]

By the mid-seventies, factors such as improvement in birth control, more favorable attitudes toward working women and increased life expectancy led many women back to work outside the home.

---

[1] Lenz and Myerhoff, *Feminization of America*, 77-8.

[2] Schor, *Overworked American*, 95.

How It Is: Women in the Home and Workplace

THE POSITION, SALARY AND TYPE OF WORK in which women engage has not changed equally with the increase in their employment. Women earn sixty-seven cents for every dollar men earn. Forty percent of working women earn less than $10,000 a year. Over half of all families living below poverty level are headed by women. Women are most likely to work in white collar clerical positions (pink ghettos) or service occupations, which totals almost fifty-five percent of all women's employment. In 1987, women represented eighty percent of all administrative support, sixty-nine percent of retail and personal service sales, and thirty-eight percent of executives, managers and administrators. Today, women at work need access to health- and childcare, higher wages and more flexible working conditions to balance work and family.

- 74% of men work.

- 79% of women with no children under eighteen work; 67% of women with children work.

- Nearly 75% of all working mothers are married.

- Four out of five divorced women with children under eighteen are in the labor force.[3]

Effects of the Baby Boom Generation: The baby boom generation has made a striking impact on the world of work. Indulged as they grew up, boomers believe that their opportunities are endless. They are more educated and more affluent than their parents. Baby boomers comprise one third of the population and are the fastest-growing segment of the labor force. The baby boom attitude regarding work differs from that of their predecessors. Work is no longer a chore completed to earn a paycheck. Boomers are looking for

---

[3] National Commission on Working Women, "Women's Work Force Network of Wider Opportunities for Women" (Fall/Winter 1991-92).

careers, challenges and flexible workstyles. More and more are seeking self-expression and personal gratification from work. When self-esteem is intact, fewer are willing to accept the values and structures of the traditional work environments. As more seek alternatives, and as more speak out, work environments will begin to transform.

Partially due to the glut of qualified workers, industries are also changing. As layers of management have been eliminated, positions no longer go to all of those qualified. Rather than moving up a vertical path, boomers are navigating horizontal paths within a company, switching companies, going out on their own, or changing careers. Some have chosen to downshift to lower positions and live less stressful lifestyles. These shifts align with the values of life quality and self-expression baby boomers are seeking.

How It Could Be: Success and Balance

BETWEEN NOW AND THE YEAR 2,000, women will fill two thirds of all new positions; in other words, twice as many women are entering the workforce as are men. Women's number in the labor force will rise from fifty-six million to sixty-six million. In the last two decades, the number of women working as professionals has increased from ten to forty percent. The percentage of women physicians has doubled, and the percentage of women lawyers and architects has nearly quintupled. Close to one third of all computer scientists are women. One third of all the MBA's granted are to women. According to the Small Business Association, women own thirty percent of all small businesses, and they start two out of every three new businesses.[4]

As more women enter the workforce, the male-dominated corporate structure will shift, and a more feminine structure will amend the way business is done. In the seventies and early eighties, women were

---

[4] Naisbitt and Aburdene, *Megatrends 2000*, 224.

trying to become part of this predominantly male environment. *The Plateauing Trap, The Gamesman,* and *Up the Organization* were popular book titles. In the eighties, books such as *Sequencing, The Super Woman, Habits of the Heart,* and *Feminine Leadership or How To Succeed in Business Without Being One of the Boys* emerged. These topics reflect the need for more a humane work environment.

Women and Leadership: Women's ways of working, such as mutuality, cooperation and affiliation, are becoming recognized as healthier ways to work with people. We can empower ourselves and others by using our preferred mode of operating and by not trying to imitate masculine styles of leadership. Then, not only will working conditions change, but so will leadership in business change. Old-style management in industry is much like the hierarchy of the military model, which fit well into an industrial economy. Work was task-oriented, mechanical and outer-directed. Close supervision was important. Technological advancements and the information industry has changed work from muscle-power to brain-power. The typical industrial worker is stoic, physical, pragmatic and inexpressive, while the typical modern worker is expressive, nurturing, intuitive and cooperative. Work is what people think, imagine, synthesize, exchange in a meeting and communicate to others. Collaboration and compromise will and must replace competition and rivalry.

The new industry, along with baby boom values and feminine workstyles, has created not only a gender of new workers but a generation of new workers and new leaders. Work values of firmness, competition, and external power are shifting to teamwork, self-expression and mutuality. Thus, leaders of these new workers must also change. An authoritarian type will not suit the new worker. Words like "teacher," "coach," and "mentor" more appropriately describe new leaders. Those who know how to draw out the strengths from others, how to guide people, and how to demonstrate or role model appropriate behavior or action are needed.[5] Women

---

[5] Naisbitt and Aburdene, *Megatrends 2000,* 227.

have used these characteristics in the traditionally "female" work environments of childcare, education and nursing.

Work environments are becoming more democratic; each person's unique skills and personality are acknowledged and put to use for the benefit of the greater whole. In these settings, teamwork and win-win/positive interpersonal relations are recognized as contributing to better work relationships, which lead to greater productivity. As long as women realize that they do not need to lose their feminine sides, they can carry over these traits into any setting in which they choose to work. As women in the workforce hold dear their feminine qualities and integrate these with their masculine qualities, they will engender a healthier, happier and more productive workforce.

Those who are dubious about promises of a changing work ethic, take note that this metamorphosis will be gradual and will occur only with the collective support from working women and men. Women over forty formulated their career goals in a world where women were a minority. Chances are they set their goals according to the old standards. Women under forty have new visions and expectations that can change the environment for future workers.

Changing Roles in the Family: Both men and women are seeking balance between career and family. In a 1992 survey, seventy-five percent of women and sixty-nine percent of men said they would take a pay cut or pass up a promotion to spend more time with their children. According to a 1989 survey, eighty-two percent of women and seventy-eight percent of men said they would choose flexible hours and slower advancement over inflexible hours and more advancement. Four out of five fathers are now in the delivery room at the births of their children, and sixty-two percent of prospective fathers attend childbirth classes with their wives. Fifty-eight percent help take care of babies, sixty percent change diapers, and sixty-seven percent feed their babies. Twenty-four percent of new mothers who planned to go back to work said their

16

husbands will take care of the child.[6] As men and women join in changing perceptions regarding family responsibilities (or what is considered women's work) and what is the appropriate workstyle and work environment, a balance of roles in the workplace and at home is conceivable.

Childcare: National leaders' attitudes and policies regarding mothers at work do not reflect what is actually occurring in the workforce. Statisticians predict that by the year 2,000, eighty- four percent of women in childbearing age will be working. The average yearly expense of childcare costs runs $3,000 per child. Slowly, employers are recognizing and accommodating dual-career families by providing childcare tax breaks, childcare in the workplace and childcare options in benefit packages. Some of the nation's biggest companies are showing sensitivity to families. For instance, Apple Computer runs an inhouse daycare and gives $500 to each employee's new baby. IBM grants new mothers leaves up to three years with benefits and guarantees jobs. Meek and Company has donated land and money for a childcare facility and allows mothers to work at home. Hewlett-Packard allows employees to start between 6 and 8:30 A.M. and leave between 2:30 and 5 P.M. Stride Rite opened the nation's first childcare center in 1971. Patagonia has an onsite childcare center and offers childcare for ages eight weeks to fourteen years. Pacific Bell has helped employees set up offices with computer terminals in their homes. Olsten Temporary Agency offers a childcare benefit plan in which temporary employees can elect to have all or part of their childcare expenses deducted from their paychecks and reduce their taxable income. The money is reimbursed in a separate tax-free check.

Other companies subsidize the cost of childcare. Employees contribute part of their salary; they do not pay income or social security tax on the money set aside, which can save from fifteen to twenty-eight percent in taxes. Since 1989, California companies have received a tax credit of up to $30,000 for starting childcare centers. Many city

---

[6] Lenz and Myerhoff, *Feminization of America,* 113.

and county planners now require developers to pay fees for new projects to fund improvements to existing childcare facilities or to construct new facilities.

Yet this is only the beginning. Government leaders and employers must face that women are in the workforce to stay. Families with both parents working must address their childcare concerns to leaders and employers for conditions to change.

Alternative Workstyles: As a result of changes in attitudes regarding work and the demographics of the labor force, both employers and workers are examining new workstyles. Options such as part-time employment, contract work and permanent part-time staff are emerging. Flextime, including such options as compressed work-weeks, jobsharing, and work-at-home arrangements, is becoming a trend in the U.S. workforce.

Alternative workstyles may actually become the norm. Competition in a global market is forcing companies to trim down, and individuals not part of the central core necessary to run a company are no longer needed on a full-time basis. Managers, for instance, are not required to supervise assemblers, and factory workers have been replaced by machines or computers. Our economy has shifted from manufacturing to providing information and services. About eighty percent of all work are service jobs, and about forty percent of all jobs are information oriented. Companies need people for technical skills, for specific knowledge or expertise, and for thinking and communication skills, as in troubleshooting and creative problem-solving. These skills are not usually needed on a continuous basis but for various projects or for stages in a company's operation.

As a consequence, according to Charles Handy, author of *The Age of Unreason*, the world or work is changing into a three-ringed circle. The inner ring consists of managers, marketing strategists, technicians and salespeople. The inner core of this ring is similar to the conventional executive staffing in corporations, except that this group includes fewer people.

18

The outer ring consists of interchangeable workers who may or may not have regular, full-time positions with the company. This ring includes both skilled and non-skilled clerical and hourly employees who have traditionally been at the bottom of the hierarchy and payscale. Many of these people are hired as temporary or part-time help, most likely through temporary agencies.

The middle ring contains "portfolio people," who have contracts with corporations for their services and/or expertise. Contract portfolio people will work for several companies rather than move up the career ladder in one company. These people need to be flexible, creative and able to draw on a variety of skills which can be marketed to possible employers. Portfolio people may work in one or more fields and/or in one or more industries, offering a variety of skills. They might work an intense six months to complete one project followed by several months off. Or they may contract part-time work for different companies at the same time. Portfolio people must be able to realize their various skills and market these through samples of their work, much like an artist does. Portfolio workers are self-managers of their time and their careers. The attributes of portfolio workers fit well with many women's workstyles because women still tend to carry most of the responsibility of home/children and maintain several undertakings. Portfolio work calls for flexibility, juggling and self-management. The disadvantages of this type of work are the lack of job security and benefits.

Both portfolio workers and the outer-ring temporary workers will need to find sources other than their employers for their benefits. These sources will include temporary agencies, unions, professional organizations, local or community organizations, and the government.

Work at Home: The term "worksteading" is used to describe individuals who leave their offices to work at home. With the advent of telecommunications, including fax and personal computers, much more business can be done from the home. In the past, women have preferred to work at home because doing so was the only possible income-producing option available. They had jobs such as running boarding houses, dressmaking and doing piecework. Today, approximately one million U.S. women work from the home.[7] Within thirty years, nearly one third of the workforce may telecommute at least part-time. Already, over twenty-six million men and women, or one quarter of the labor force, has moved part to all of their work to the home.[8] A conservative estimate shows a twenty-percent increase in productivity for those who move their work into the home. Worksteaders show a lower turnover rate and zero absenteeism. Most corporate work-at-home jobs are those with telecommuting capabilities in which companies set up employees with computers and other necessities. Worksteading prevails in fields such as real estate, publishing, insurance, pharmaceuticals, apparel, cosmetics, sales and printing.

If you are planning to move your work to your home, make sure your family members (including spouses) understand the boundaries concerning your workspace and time. You must also discipline yourself to stay away from running errands or doing a load of laundry instead of your non-household work. A problem that frequently arises with those who work at home are not the stay-away boundaries but the when-to-stop boundaries. Thus, a clearly defined work schedule that keeps you working when you should be and not working when you should not be is essential.

Jobsharing: My introduction to the concept of jobsharing occurred in 1979. I met an elementary school teacher who alternated workweeks with another teacher. Since then, I have met women attorneys, doctors, forest rangers, accountants, secretaries, counselors and business managers who are jobsharing. These women divide the duties, responsibilities, salary and benefits of their respective positions with another person. Jobsharing programs are offered by nearly twenty percent of U.S. companies.

---

[7] Lenz and Myerhoff, *Feminization of America*, 92.

[8] Roxane Farmanfarmaian, "Worksteading—The New Lifestyle Frontier," *Psychology Today* (November 1989): 37.

If you already have a job that you would like to share, your first important task is to find the appropriate partner. Good communication skills and getting along are imperative. As if you were recruiting for any other position, solicit the best candidate for the job by advertising for and interviewing applicants.

Applying for a new job as a team this will be more difficult because you must convince the employer—to whom you have not yet proven a track record—that you and your partner combined are the best candidates for the job. Therefore, document the advantages of hiring two rather than one employee, outline your shared responsibilities by defining each partner's area of strength and emphasis, and assign the major and minor roles each of you will take for each of your job duties. Be sure to determine how benefits will be divided.[9]

Because persuading employers who do not have jobsharing programs can be trying, you must demonstrate how the advantages to the employer more than outweigh the disadvantages. Include the following jobsharing benefits from the employer's perspective:

- greater flexibility
- reduction in turnover
- wider range of skills in one job
- greater energy on the job
- reduction in absenteeism
- continuity of job performance
- more alert and less stressful employees
- no need for extra staffing during peak periods

Non-Traditional Careers: Although some effort has been made to recruit women in male-dominated occupations, women tend not to enter scientific, mechanical and technological careers and occupations in large numbers. Only nine percent of working women are

---

[9] Lee, *Complete Guide to Job Sharing*, 30-45.

in non-traditional occupations. Nearly half of the wage gap between men and women can be attributed to sex segregation among occupations. Women do not enter non-traditional occupations because of male-female stereotyping and because they lack exposure in these fields. Women born before the early years of the civil rights era were already influenced by the stereotyping of women's work.

As new generations of females grow up expecting to enter into careers, they must consider more alternatives prior to selecting occupations. They must evaluate their ideas about male-dominated occupations. For instance, what are the similarities between tiling a floor and making a patchwork quilt? Women sometimes feel awkward using power tools, yet most of the tools and equipment used in traditional female worksettings are power-operated machines. The difference is in the training and belief system regarding what is women's work and what is men's work. In the past, parents and educators have reinforced stereotypes, and women lack female role models in these fields. However, their attitudes are changing about the type of work they are able to perform. Those women entering non-traditional fields serve as role models. Consider non-traditional alternatives when you are exploring options. Scholarships, government programs and women's networks exist to encourage and aid women in entering these fields. Interview others already in the field to learn about their challenges and to gain support.

CHAPTER II

Career Development for Women

Opportunities to develop a career did not exist for many people at the turn of this century, and career choice was the luxury of few. Many men followed their fathers' footsteps or "fell" into jobs. They typically remained in the same jobs throughout their lives, and those who did not were considered unstable. Married women, on the other hand, were not expected to take on jobs and became homemakers.

Over the years, society's concept of work has changed, and views on adulthood have shifted from that of a fixed and settled stage to one with considerable growth and transformation. In adulthood, one's vocation is a major consideration. "Career development" has been defined as a series of related jobs, usually up a hierarchy and within an organization, or with different organizations. Salary increases, recognition and more freedom to pursue one's own interest or select one's projects are some motivations for advancement. Due to the constant changes in technology, jobs are no longer static nor secure. Society's attitudes regarding work and life are also altering. Current theories of adult development include information on career development. However, most research is based on the development of men, not women.

How Women's Career Development Differs

BECAUSE THE DECISION TO MARRY AND/OR have children is an integral part of adult life, committing to a career is not as simple for women as it is for men. A woman must consider the timing of children, childcare responsibilities, leaving and reentering the workforce, and integrating a career with that of her spouse. Income and social interaction are the two most important factors for women choosing work outside the home. For many, the opportunity for advancement and personal growth is nearly non-existent. Women, generally, receive more rewards from home and family. Many choose occupations that require little commitment and that are low in stress level so they can offer their best to their families. Others do not work outside the home for money, instead becoming involved in the children's school and athletic extra-curricular activities or participating in community or charity work. Women who do pursue careers often delay starting families. They then find themselves pressured by their biological clocks, unsure whether they can, or even want to, do both. All these issues must be addressed in the career development of women.

For both men and women, the new definition of "career development" will more closely resemble that of personal development. In order to find the best career fit, men and women must first understand and decide what they want from life. Men can learn from women because the female gender, due to its precarious role in the workforce, has been more creative in choosing work patterns and has not conformed to the rigid and linear career patterns men set for themselves. Women can create their own, flexible, open, more gratifying pattern since they are on the edge of a new work ethic. Current career development philosophy emphasizes doing what you love and finding a work-life balance; it defines work as a form of self-expression. This view transforms the old definition and parameters of work. If women proceed with this new focus, they will have a greater chance of having all their needs met than by trying to fit into the old male patterns. Men, as well, will be making this shift because their roles and personal development are changing along with women's.

Men and women need to clarify their priorities and separate their desires from the "shoulds" they learned. Typical shoulds for women are: "I should be home with my kids." "I should let my husband's career come first." "I should go to work and be a perfect homemaker." Typical shoulds for men are: "I should try for that promotion even though I like where I am." "I should continue this job I don't like because it's secure."

Women need to identify whether they want careers, whether they want to work outside of the home, or whether they want some combination thereof. They need to think about the possibility of taking a break in employment to have children. They need to decide what lifestyle they desire. These concerns are as important as deciding whether to become a nurse, a computer programmer or business owner.

When considering these ideas, women can put together a workable plan that will combine their dreams, abilities, interests, values and personality with marriage, family, mortgages, leisure and continued growth.

General Stages of Development

THE FIVE STAGES OF WOMEN'S DEVELOPment are loosely formed and do not follow the linear path scholars hypothesized in the past. There is no predictable sequence to the process, nor is there a timetable. Maturation is affected by internal and external, biological and environmental, cultural and situational, economical and personal factors. Any combination or all of these factors will influence women's development at any time.

Each stage of life—childhood, adolescence, early adulthood, middle adulthood and later adulthood—contains some typical issues to resolve and tasks to complete. Life seems to happen whether or not matters are resolved or tasks are completed, and people do not usually work out all their issues before entering the next stage. Often, unresolved concerns will plague people until these issues are confronted. For example, many women enter the adult world without a strong sense of identity or self-esteem. Often they marry before they have developed their own identities, thus latching on to their role as wife of Mr. Smith and mother of Johnny. When Johnny moves away, or husbands leave through death or divorce, women are left desolate, with no identity of their own.

Transition Periods:

> A transition is a natural process of disorientation and reorientation that alters the perception of self and the world and demands changes in assumptions and behavior...(It) is a process of reconstruction affecting the interiority of the self—identity and being, values and feelings, and thinkings. Transformation occurs from the inside out.[1]

According to Daniel Levinson (*Seasons of a Man's Life*), adulthood is not static. Adults alternate between constant periods and growth periods throughout life. The transition phase creates change, and during the stable phase people live with those changes. Transitions do not have a timetable, nor do they necessarily occur between stages of development. Passage from stable to transition may be caused by internal developments, such as turning forty and realizing that half of life has passed by. Often, however, changes are caused by external prompts, such as needing to find employment and new social outlets because of a divorce, or deciding to suspend a career to stay home and raise children.

---

[1] Hudson, *Adult Years*, 96.

A major transition issue for many women is the loss of financial security due to divorce or death of their spouse. Many women are heads of household and must work either at home or outside the home plus attend children with little or no help from the children's fathers. Whether already working outside the home or not, these women's career choices will be influenced by opportunities for money and security. Therefore, many times, their career search is oriented toward jobs that require little training and offer financial security. The idea of finding careers they love seems like an unattainable dream. For instance, although Maria had ambitions to become a nurse or teacher, when she and her husband separated, she took a job as a receptionist. Maureen chose a career path that would provide security and benefits. Later, some women will encounter another transition period in which they may consider new career options that not only fulfill financial needs but also more personal, expressive needs.

Whatever the cause or reason, we experience a conversion, which produces emotional and psychic strain in which we make major decisions about the future and about ourselves. Often, we seek answers or outside help at these times. Or we become more spiritual as we look for answers and relief. During these periods we make minor or major adjustments and continue with our lives, moving toward the next transition period. In most instances, both internal and external matters occur simultaneously. Shifts can occur at any time during any stage to agitate our lives. How we view this disturbance is the key.

Childhood: Establishing a sense of trust and esteem are children's main concerns. Children evolve by relating to their families and the adult world. In childhood, we discover our own uniqueness and hope to be loved for who we are. To some degree, the environment influences who we become, but we enter the world with an integral nature. How our nature develops depends upon life experiences and the way the we interpret those events. We need approval from adults and our peers, and we need to feel valued.

Childhood experiences have a major impact on adulthood. Thus, comprehending and accepting our childhood is vital to our adult experience. Identity and self-esteem are based on personal history. Sifting the environmental influences from our inner core is important in understanding ourselves and in determining our futures more clearly. Our profile character Paula, for instance, adapted her natural behavior to seek approval from her stepfather by being a good girl and curbing her expressive nature.

Boys and girls have divergent influences during childhood. Girls emerge from persons like themselves, while boys emerge from persons who are different.

> [F]or boys and men, separation and individuation are critically tied to gender identity since separation from the mother is essential for the development of masculinity. For girls and women,...feminine identity [does] not depend on the achievement of separation from the mother or on the progress of individuation.[2]

As a result, women seek identification with, rather than separation from, people. Men relate to the world out of separation and detachment, and women want to share, relate and empathize. Boys are encouraged to be active and rational, while girls are encouraged to be in touch with feelings and relationships. Events are satisfying to women when they increase their emotional connection with others.[3] In a man's world, however, these feminine strengths of relating and cooperating are not valued equally with the masculine ones of rationality, competition and activity. Thus, women often feel at a disadvantage. For instance, another profile character, Maureen, being the only girl with four brothers, saw herself handicapped in a male environment of rationality, competition and activity. She denied her feminine side as a child and throughout her adulthood.

---

[2] Gilligan, *In a Different Voice*, 8.

[3] Miller, *Toward a New Psychology of Women*, 39.

Adolescence: The themes during adolescence are identity and independence. Our bodies and emotions are changing. We learn that there is not only one way of "becoming." We make decisions regarding beliefs, friends, interests and values.

Modern society has evolved into an elaborate life structure. Unlike our human ancestors, whose primary concerns consisted of basic needs such as food and shelter, in advanced cultures children spend about twelve school years in preparation for survival. Basic needs have expanded to include multi-roomed dwellings, automobiles, electronic gadgets to perform (now- considered) tedious household chores. Work is no longer directly related to survival needs and is exchanged for symbolic rewards that provide the means to exist. Written laws depict right from wrong. Religion edifies morals. Madison Street exposes the material items necessary to exist. Culture explicates how to behave and think and separates individual groups from other groups. Economic developments and world events affect future survival. Many of the these institutions represent conflicting beliefs. Life is extremely complex for adolescents and young adults who are yet exploring their ideas and ideals in order to exist in this world.

The major concern for adolescent girls is social development. In prehistoric times, families were loosely formed around blood relatives, and labor was divided for convenience. Mates were selected by elders for economic and political reasons. Only in recent history and in some cultures are mates chosen for love. A great deal of confusion revolves around the concept of romantic love. Often young women and men seek their mates not out of love, but because they need to be loved or they need to fill a gap that was not filled during childhood. Traditionally, boys were raised to become breadwinners, and girls were raised to become mothers and wives dependent on the bread- winners. Women's identities, thus, are contingent on their success with the opposite sex. Profile characters Maria and Paula were much more concerned with dating and their social lives than in contemplating careers.

Although the need to depend on men for physical survival no longer exists, finding a mate is often of utmost importance. Feminism has partially changed women's perspectives, but advertising, laws, and religion espouse women as dependent beings. The key issue for the adolescent female, hereunto, is attracting a mate, followed by thinking about a career. And career decisions have become more complex than "What shall I do when I grow up?" Imperative questions include: "What will be my primary goal in life—work or family, or both? If I decide on a career, how and when will I fit in a family? Whose career will have priority, mine or my mate's? Is it possible for both our careers to have preference? If I choose to follow a traditional course, will I be fulfilled, and what will people think of me? What is the appropriate role and behavior for a woman?"

In becoming young adults, our first transition occurs during late adolescence. We are anxiously involved with identity and independence. Girls in their late teens strive to understand who they are aside from the assigned roles of daughter, student, sister and girlfriend. Adolescents separate their own values from those of their parents, culture and society. They strive to become independent of parents, to separate from family, and to formulate their own ideas. They make decisions about the future and about their adult roles. They establish their internal feminine and masculine roles and identity. They interact with peers and reaffirm their relations to the same or opposite sex.

Early Adulthood: In this period, people actively participate in the adult world through experimenting, choosing, deciding, and consuming. The core and substance of early adulthood focuses on the external. They may not know what their choosing, becoming and developing will lead to. They deal with the residue of their upbringing, circumstances, environment, current needs, feelings, thoughts and beliefs. As is often said, "If I only knew then what I know now." But we don't. Eventually we will reassess some of those early decisions.

Adulthood normally begins with leaving the core family in order to live and work independently. People take on tasks and responsibilities that contribute to the workforce or to society. Adulthood includes autonomous decision-making, financial independence, coupling, forming our own values and life calling. Often, women who marry young do not acquire a sense of independence because their decision-making is not sovereign and their financial security comes from their husbands. As a result, these women may not perceive themselves as capable of surviving without their mates and may suffer repercussions as a result. Maria, who moved directly from her family's home into a marriage, did not feel independent until she took a job at the age of twenty-five. By then, she had two children. Paula is confounded because her role as mother no longer exists and she lacks a new adult role.

Women who work at home must recognize that they contribute in laboring, nurturing, planning, organizing, managing, creating and in all the other feats of managing a household. They do not believe that they can join the laborforce because they lack work experience. Employers maintain this position by not hiring women who lack employment histories. For this very reason, Paula finds it difficult to enter the "world of work." This notion is misleading and will be discussed in chapter five, "Skills: Inventory Your Experiences."

Whether career-oriented or home-oriented, married women frequently do not consider their own activity as important as that of their husbands. When women do pursue their self-interests, they have difficulty allowing this kind of activity to be a basis of their worth.[4] Women can recognize another's needs and serve these needs more readily than their own. Women respond to others' needs without feeling that it diminishes their sense of identity.[5] In result, women develop the belief that their "own needs, even though unexamined, untested and unexpressed will somehow be fulfilled in return."[6] For instance, Maria believed that her husband would love her more because she served him so well. The tragedy is that he felt trapped and the marriage ended.

---

[4] Miller, *Toward a New Psychology of Women*, 54.

[5] Ibid., 62.

[6] Ibid., 65.

Many women are joining men in "masculine" aspirations to fulfill themselves. The contest for women such as Maureen is difficult because they have few role models to show the way, and tradition prescribes that women's main duties are to be wives and mothers. Even as a single parent, Maureen chose not to accept promotions she desired because they required long hours away from her children.

Some women, married or unmarried, find satisfaction in pursuing their personal aspirations in a context that serves the needs of their families. Paula chose to help her husband with his work but did not allow herself her own career because she didn't want to be selfish. Maureen eventually convinced herself to take on a promotion after the children became more independent because of her financial needs.

Other women, particularly those who are economically independent, have no use for the archetype of a traditional marriage in which "man" is the breadwinner and "wife" attends home and children. Women who have their own career interests and economic security may not choose this archetypal marriage, instead seeking other ways to have relationships. These women may encounter judgment by both men and women with conventional views. Such judgments could impact a woman's career opportunities. The profile character Sara, in traditional thinking, would be called a "spinster" because she is middle-aged and has never been married. Sara wants children but is not interested in marriage. Instead, she is considering artificial insemination in order to become pregnant.

Today, many lifestyle alternatives exist, and contemporary views support that marriage is not always the answer, nor are children for everyone. Women are beginning to find other means for self-expression, and often it is in their careers.

Middle Adulthood: By this time, the outer tasks such as establishing careers and/or family and a sense of self have normally been accomplished. At middle adulthood, we become more introverted and peer inward with philosophical, religious, and spiritual means in order to understand the meaning of life. We continue to accomplish, generate and contribute, while yearning to internalize and assess our past. At midlife, less time remains to change or modify. Fulfilled and content or not, there is room for growth. For those with children, roles have changed within the family because the children have grown and left. Roles also change with aging parents, who often become more dependant.

Much fun has been poked at the middle-aged person acting like a teenager. This seemingly unusual behavior comes out of the need to reevaluate values, skills, interests, and identity. Middle-aged people temporarily return to their adolescent-like concerns. But this time, they form judgments based on life experiences. The key issues of this stage are accepting one's self and one's life. The questions to ask are:

- Do I accept my life, accomplishments, mates, children, parents, jobs as they are?

- If not, what am I going to do about it?

- Am I going to regret what has happened, or am I going to redefine and modify?

- And how do I accomplish all of the above?"

Those in their mid-thirties to mid-forties who have had children early are ready to expand their lives with a new meaning. Many baby boom women have waited until their thirties or forties to begin families. Immersed in careers and prompted by biological clocks, they contemplate balancing maternal needs and the responsibilities of their careers. Or they quit jobs in order to watch and nurture their youngsters. Others may choose not to have children. Those with older children may gain new freedom and leisure time and enter or reenter the workforce. Paula, having been a homemaker for over twenty years, is perplexed at what to do with the rest of her life. Maria, in her mid-twenties, is juggling her head-of-household, mother and employee roles. Maureen, a long-time single working mom, has new freedom and opportunities and role changes within her family. Sara's biological clock continues to tick as she approaches midlife.

A Note about Mothers: The adult development of mothers could be viewed as the changing of seasons. Spring represents the birth of children and the early years of childraising. Summer is the period when children are maturing and when mothers give emotionally, physically and spiritually. When the children are grown and have moved away, mothers find themselves bereaved unless they are prepared for autumn. Then they have time to think about their own selves. It can be a period for tremendous internal growth. These mothers are young enough to make contributions to the outside world or to their inner world, as they choose. The winter season will depend on how mothers make use of our fall harvest. With a bounteous fall, mothers can enjoy the winter season.[7]

Later Adulthood:

> [T]here is no need for us to take upon ourselves the responsibility of sheltering the very old from worry....That is no kindness to the old. Rather it is cruelty because it deprives them of their power to grow. It is an unpardonable belittling of the role of the aged, for it is they who, whether they can formulate it or not, are in fact the depositories of wisdom.[8]

Unlike other cultures, Americans do not appreciate their elders. Older people lose status with their children, in the community and at work. They seek respect, independence and the nearness of loved ones. They want to understand the changing world and have others listen to how it was. They become concerned about death and afterlife and loneliness. They want to achieve integrity; they want to accept their pasts and themselves. They take up new interests and hobbies, or they become involved in charitable work. They continue to introspect and become less concerned with proving themselves. They can be gentler, more humanitarian and patient with others and with themselves.

---

[7] de Castillejo, *Knowing Woman*, 149-164.

[8] Ibid., 163.

When is later adulthood? Is it after midlife or after the children have grown? For many men and women, later adulthood represents almost half a lifetime. For men and some women, retirement is the major indicator of the end of life. For women, late adulthood often means that the children have moved away and started their own families. Yet, some may only be in their thirties or forties when this occurs! Getting beyond the "empty nest syndrome" offers a new sense of freedom. Suddenly, older adults have leisure time. They might initially take on jobs to fill the time that can provide an outlet for expression. If they have held jobs outside the home, they have the opportunity to commit further to work. Many begin their careers in their forties and fifties. Or they may return to school, obtain degrees, and then pursue careers. Others, because of separation from spouses through divorce or death, suddenly find themselves concerned with career issues during middle or late adulthood.

With traditional views of age, older women find it difficult to confidently enter job markets, not to mention the fears of not being considered an equal because they are women. For those with established careers, the pattern will be more similar to that of men, which includes plateauing, declining, restructuring and self-renewal.

A reformation of attitudes toward older adults, in general, is on its way. In a new age—with both men and women working in and out of the home, with life expectancy increases, with better overall health, and with the advent of the baby boom bulge—America will see a major change in attitudes toward older adults because the bulk of the population will be "old." The women of the twenty-first century will have new challenges at midlife and later adulthood. Women will start businesses and professional careers or completely change their careers. Some of those who committed to careers in their twenties and thirties may later stay home to have children and find alternative workstyles as the children grow. Many with children will take work into the home. Traditional homemakers will continue to contribute with volunteer work, philanthropy or using their well-earned skills in similar settings for pay. Older men and women will work in jobs that normally are filled by young adults or teenagers. The younger "old folks" will help with the elderly and in many humanitarian and service-oriented positions.

Both men and women need to broaden their perspective of late adulthood. If we change our views on what it means to be old, we can realize and know that we have much potential and much to offer our world, whether it is through a vocation or an avocation. Then we can move toward integrity and not feel despair that life is over and we have nothing left to offer. Give back integrity to old folks, and maybe we can become wise old people in our culture.

Exercises

A. Your Life History

Your first exercise is to write an autobiography. Writing about yourself stimulates what lies dormant in your unconscious and crystallizes your thoughts and feelings. Don't focus on the inane details such as the names of your schools or the hospital in which you were born, but remember special moments during your childhood. For instance, I remember going clothes shopping with my mom, sharing my secret fantasy land with my dad, and being excited about an upcoming move. Include in your history times of distress and of frustration. My family moved frequently and I often had to change schools, not only from year to year, but within the same schoolyear. I sometimes had difficulty making new friends and leaving old friends. Be sure to include achievements such as doing well in school, winning a contest, or overcoming obstacles. Include accomplishments and disappointments of your adult life. Think about what led you to where you are today.

Answer these questions:

- What interested you as a kid and young adult?

- What were some of your life ambitions?

- Who were the people that impressed you and/or influenced you the most?

- How and why did these people have an influence on you?

- What distracted you from your dreams and ambitions?

- Why did you change your mind about affairs?

As you are writing this history, try to detect a theme to your life. Notice which events made you feel successful, accomplished and which raised your self-esteem. Notice the events that were difficult, produced conflict and were disappointing. Is there a pattern?

When writing your autobiography, keep in mind the stages of development described in this chapter.

- What stage are you in now?

- What issues do you need to resolve from present or past stages, and how will you do so?

B. Your Life Mission

Review your autobiography for a theme, essence or principal of what your life is about. Imagine that you possess powers to discern the meaning of your life. Write out the script.

- What is your life mission?

- What are your lessons?

- What are the gifts you have come here to share?

Note: The following exercises are a warmup for the next chapter; if possible, complete them before moving on.

C. Describe Yourself

1. Describe yourself in a paragraph or two. For help with using descriptive words, refer to Table 1: Personality Traits, page 40.

2. Ask someone who knows you well to describe you.

3. What traits do you like about yourself? What traits do you dislike about yourself?

4. What type of people do you admire? Why? What type of people do you envy? Why?

5. What is your fantasy job/career? What characteristics do people in that profession have? Which of those characteristics do you possess?

D. Uncover the Real You

To begin, use the relaxation exercise in the appendix.

Think about a time and place in your life in which you felt totally comfortable with yourself. Return to a time when you were not playing a role and when you felt that you could express the real you. This may be when you were very young. It may be a certain period in your life. It may be when you were around a certain person (who allowed you to be who you were). It may be a certain situation or activity in which you were engrossed.

Clearly imagine that time and place. Use all your senses. Picture your surroundings. What do you see? smell? hear? Who are you with? What are you doing? Imagine yourself completely comfortable and content at what you are doing.

When you are ready, conclude this memory and write a description of the setting, including what you did and who was there. List some adjectives that characterize you in this memory.

Table 1: Personality Traits

Abstract: Theoretical, not practical or easily understood.

Aesthetic: Enjoy being surrounded by or creating beauty.

Altruistic: Involved in helping others; humanistic.

Analytical: Enjoy reasoning by separating into parts or basic principles so as to determine the whole.

Aspiring: Often have grand ambitions.

Careful: Prefer to be cautious in thought, speech or action.

Charismatic: Able to draw devotion from groups of people.

Charitable: Generous in giving help to needy.

Cognitive: Enjoy acquiring knowledge and reasoning.

Collaborative: Enjoy working with others in joint effort.

Communicative: Inclined to communicate easily.

Complex: Often have involved, intricate or complicated thoughts and ideas.

Conceptual: Often use thoughts, ideas or notions.

Concrete: Prefer dealing with things perceptible to the senses or that exist in real experience.

Congenial: Extend warmth, friendliness and cordiality.

Constant: Am unchanging in nature and steadfast in purpose.

Contemplative: Like to ponder and consider thoughtfully.

Controlled: Prefer holding restraint.

Creative: Able to develop or invent with originality.

Discerning: Often perceive the obscure and concealed.

Dominant: Able to rule.

Earthy: Am hearty, down-to-earth, uninhibited.

Economical: Prudent in management of money or resources.

Efficient: Usually act or produce with minimum waste, expense or unnecessary effort.

Empathetic: Intimately understand the thoughts, feelings and motives of others.

Expressive: Like to express my feelings or opinions through words, art, music or movement.

Extravagant: Enjoy expending lavishly, having excess and abundance.

Formal: Prefer doing things in proper form; enjoy ceremony.

Gracious: Am courteous and hospitable.

Hands-On: Enjoy working with my hands.

Helping: Enjoy aiding, contributing or offering assistance.

Hospitable: Am open to strangers and enjoy entertaining.

Idealistic: Believe in possibilities and visions.

Table 1: Personality Traits (continued)

Imaginative: Readily create mental concepts or visions.

Influential: Enjoy affecting people or course of events.

Ingenious: Have inventive or imaginative mind.

Intellectual: Enjoy engaging my mind.

Introspective: Enjoy turning my thoughts inward and examining myself.

Investigative: Enjoy observing or inquiring in detail, or examining systematically.

Leading: Enjoy commanding or guiding others.

Literal: Prefer taking things word for word; concerned with facts.

Logical: Prefer to reason through systematic and linear manner.

Mechanical: Enjoy making, using or repairing machines and tools.

Merciful: Am compassionate and lenient.

Methodical: Possess ordered and systematic habits of behavior.

Non-conformist: Dislike being bound by accepted rules, beliefs or practices.

Nurturing: Like to promote development of others.

Organized: Like to structure, order or arrange.

Perfectionist: Have propensity for extremely high standards.

Personable: Am easy to know and get along with.

Persuasive: Easily able to win over others to a course of action by reasoning or inducement.

Physical: Enjoy physical activity and being fit.

Poised: Easily composed and free from embarrassment.

Pragmatic: Enjoy being active rather than contemplative; practical-minded.

Prestigious: Enjoy prominence, status or admiration.

Prudent: Am careful about my conduct.

Reserved: Am not usually outgoing in manner or speech; undemonstrative.

Rigorous: Am firm, rugged, sturdy.

Soulful: Am full of expression or deep feeling.

Structured: Prefer organized situations and predictable outcomes.

Technical: Enjoy making, using and perfecting specialized techniques or methods.

Tolerant: Am open to the beliefs, practices or traits of others.

Traditional: Prefer to follow customs and correct modes of behavior.

Unassuming: Am not pretentious or boastful; modest.

Utilitarian: Value the practical over the aesthetic.

Visionary: Am given to speculative ideas.

Profile: Paula Dombrowski

A. My Life History

Childhood: I loved clothes. I dressed up in my mother's dresses and high heels and pretended that I was going to the ball. I was an only child, and my mother divorced before I started school. For several years it was just she and I. My stepdad was more of a father to me than my real dad.

I expressed my imagination through dancing, singing and playing theater. I didn't do well at school basics unless I really liked the teacher. This didn't go over well with my stepdad, who made me feel dumb when I couldn't get my math homework. I focused on social activities.

Adolescence: I made my own clothes and was more into my social life than my education. My heroines were mostly successful actresses who had minds of their own, like Katharine Hepburn. I wanted to be a fashion designer. When I mentioned my interests to my guidance counselor, she signed me up for home economics classes. My first real jobs were in retail stores. I enjoyed being around people. I dated a lot. I met my husband when I was twenty-one. He was decisive, strong, and attentive. I didn't have any particular goals, and getting married sounded like the thing to do.

Adulthood: I've been married for over twenty years and have three children. One is married and two are in college. For the past six years, I have helped my husband with his business. I do well with his clients. Before that, I lived the typical life of a homemaker: chauffeuring kids to baseball games and dance lessons, making cupcakes for Girl Scouts or costumes for drama club. I enjoyed being home for my children and supporting my husband.

Transition Period: My children are gone. My husband's business has grown beyond me. Now what do I do with my life? Is it possible to start a career at my age?

Paula (continued)

B. My Life Mission

In my childhood it felt good to please others. I thought little about the future. I chose my husband for his decisive and steadfast nature. I bring excitement and variety to our lives. He brings security and consistency. I was creative and expressive but had no direction. My direction became my family. My path seems to have no inner purpose. I've been fulfilling the needs of others. This is what I wanted. I don't know what I want now.

C. Describe Myself

1. Imaginative, indecisive, serving, gracious.

2. My best friend described me as creative, fun, visionary, subservient and a good listener.

3. I like being creative, imaginative, gracious, fun, visionary and a good listener. I dislike being indecisive, serving and subservient.

4. I admire those who know what they want and go for it, because that is what is hard for me. I am jealous of women who are like this, but not of men.

5. My fantasy career is being a dress designer. They must feel confident but also have artistic talent and a good business sense. I have artistic talent.

D. Uncover the Real Me

I am in my room as a teenager. Because I have a part-time job, I was able to decorate the room how I wanted it, which was pretty cool for those days. I have an area for sketching, sewing and handicrafts, which I spent much of my free time doing.

Profile: Maureen Casey

A. My Life History

Childhood and Adolescence: I was the oldest in the family and responsible for my brothers and sisters. My dad said that I was too aggressive for a girl. I think he secretly liked it. He was an alcoholic. My heroes were adventurers like Scott and Perry, who explored the Poles. I always organized activities, outings, lemonade stands, etc. I didn't realize until later that I had leadership qualities. I had a wide group of friends and was very active in high school, partially to get away from home. I could have been a good student, but girls who were smart were not popular. I wanted both worlds. I did well enough to get into college so I could leave home. My mom died rather suddenly of cancer while I was away at school. I quit school shortly after that. I didn't have specific educational goals and my classes seemed impractical.

Adulthood: I met my husband at work. I managed a coffee shop in a local ski town where he was a ski instructor. We married and had two children. I worked. He didn't. Our marriage wasn't *ever* stable, but I'm not a quitter. Then he left me. He has never been very responsible on the financial end, but he is a very warm father and spends a great deal of time with the children. Eight years ago, I became an assistant to the convention manager at the hotel. Although they offered me a sales position, which was better paying and more challenging, I remained an assistant so I would have more time for the kids. Over the years, my position grew, and now I'm the convention manager. My children are in their last years of high school. I'm engaged. My fiance lives far enough away that one of us will have to quit our jobs. I don't want to move the children from school, nor do I want to quit my job for his job. I have thought about starting my own business.

Maureen (continued)

B. My Life Mission

I was the eldest and grew up around boys to become a strong female. I have shown men at work that women can be logical, rational and assertive without being bitchy. I raised a daughter who models that balance of male and female qualities, and a son who will treat women as equals.

C. Describe Yourself

1. Strong-willed, straightforward, athletic, independent and down to earth.

2. My daughter describes me as confident, healthy, together, opinionated and assertive.

3. I like who I am.

4. I admire people who are flexible, open, hearty, dependable and intelligent.

5. My fantasy is to have my own business. I would have to work hard, be confident, take risks and be flexible. The last two are difficult for me.

D. Uncover the Real Me

I was most happy when I was in the midst of something where I would have to organize people and take care of a lot of details. This frequently occurred in high school, when I felt a strong sense of satisfaction for doing a job well.

Profile: Maria Diego

A. My Life History

Childhood and Adolescence: Our home buzzed with people and children. Someone always stopped by and children ran in and out. My mom often had her own or others' children sitting on her broad lap. I listened to the family gossip. School was not a priority, but I was a pretty good student and could have taken the more difficult college prep courses. I decided that it would be better to get practical skills than to go to college. I married my boyfriend right after school.

Early Adulthood: We had two children in four years. I tried to emulate my grandmother's marriage and home life. I had extra time when the children were in school and became a teacher's aid. I enjoyed it, but my husband didn't want me to work, so I quit. I focused on the children. I felt resentful because I wanted to work. The marriage was not going well for years before I left. My family was furious with me.

Middle Adulthood: I got a job as a receptionist in a doctor's office. As I gained confidence, I did extra work and eventually moved up to office manager. We are financially comfortable. Now I ask myself, "Is this what I want?" I would like to help people. I am unsure if I have what it takes, and am unsure I am willing to commit the time it takes for an education.

Maria *(continued)*

B. My Life Mission

This is a difficult exercise because I must look very hard at myself to see what is mine and what belongs to circumstances. Although I have always felt secure and comfortable, many people from my neighborhood have suffered difficult lives. My culture, life experiences and loving family life helped me to develop sympathy and an interest in caring for others. I like helping, caring and teaching others. With the children needing me less and with my husband gone, I don't get to care and help as much as I would like to.

C. Describe Myself

1. I'm a mother. I'm warm, friendly, helpful and love activity with people. My serious side likes to get things done efficiently. My fun side likes to tell stories and dance.

2. Mother describes me as: A strong person, hardworking, having my own mind, and helpful.

3. I like the way I get on well with people. I dislike my need to do everything perfect.

4. I admire outgoing, committed, confident and enterprising people. They are what I'd like to be.

5. A doctor would need to be outgoing, committed, confident, enterprising, helpful and love people. I have these traits, but lack confidence and am not enterprising enough.

D. Uncover the Real Me

My best time was with my grandmother. We made tortillas and picked vegetables in her garden. Once we saved an old pigeon whose wing was broken. She also told me stories from her home country about wise old medicine women.

Profile: Sara Harris

A. My Life History

Childhood and Adolescence: My whole family is talented, educated and directed. My father was an English professor and writes poetry. My mother gave up the symphony to raise us. She also painted. I had all the lessons: ballet, horseback riding, art, flute, acting. I was the youngest. My sister plays oboe for a symphony. My brother is an art history professor.

When I was little, I made doll houses, sewed clothes for my stuffed animals, wrote and performed plays. I was drawn to those in need. When I was four, we took our first trip to the city to see a musical. On the way to the theater, I saw a ragged old man with holes in his shoes sleeping on a bench. I was terrified, yet filled with compassion.

I came of age during the peace and equal rights movements and am still influenced by those times.

I had trouble choosing a major at college because I liked everything. I graduated with a double major in social work and art. I continued for a Master's in Social Work.

Adulthood: I've had several social service jobs, such as houseparent, drug rehabilitation counselor, family planning counselor and caseworker. I'm torn between wanting to work in the trenches and running away to rent a loft and paint. Social work is not what I hoped it would be. I am too idealistic. I recently entered a PhD program, thinking I might like to teach and do research. I currently work part-time as a proposal writer. It's not nearly creative enough for me and I'm afraid that college teaching will be more committees and research than I could stand. I have always ignored my creative side because it didn't seem practical to pursue it. I am thirty-nine years old, unmarried and not planning to marry. What about children?

Sara (continued)

B. My Life Mission

It seems that I have prepared for where I am heading, which is teaching college. Yet, why is my heart not in it? I envy my sister, who has committed to her craft. I don't have a craft. I never committed myself in that fashion. I would like to combine the rigors of scholarship with the intensity and creativity of the arts.

C. Describe Myself

1. Introspective, creative, intelligent, non-conforming, altruistic.

2. I've been described as heady, idealistic, serious, concerned, artistic.

3. I don't like being too serious and appear brooding.

4. I admire those who are not only creative but feel impelled to go with their vision. They have an inner strength and commitment to their work. I fear I lack in commitment and confidence.

5. Lyricist: musical, lyrical, creative, intense, committed, confident. I have the feeling but not the talent.

D. Uncover the Real Me

I'm about eight or nine at the picnic table under the oak tree in our backyard. I have the entire table filled with cut-out dolls which I'm painting. When they are done, I create a scene in which the dolls perform. I make up the script as I go along.

Part Two

Self-Assessment

CHAPTER III

Personality:
Discover Your Inner Self

In two of the exercises from chapter two—Uncover the Real You and Describe Yourself—you listed some of your personality characteristics. What is personality? The dictionary defines it as the dynamic character, self or psyche that constitutes and animates the individual person and makes her life experience unique. Your personality is the behavioral, emotional and mental expression of who you are.

Why must you examine your personality? Clearly defining your personality and characteristics helps to uncover the real you. Your personality is your unique channel for expression in which you may use your strengths and develop your weaknesses. Ideally, you will aspire to work in a setting that uses your best traits. When you are unable to express all aspects of yourself in the workplace, consider other domains, whether your personal/family life, hobbies or avocations. Because career and other life endeavors develop and change over time, you have the opportunity to embrace different aspects of yourself as you grow and transform. You must allow your career to mature as you metamorphose.

Scholars differ in their thoughts on how personality is formed. Some suggest that we are born with particular traits. Others claim that the environment determines who we become. And others state that we become who we choose to be. A combination of all these ideas has significance. We are born with a basic core which represents our underlying selves, which have several possibilities for unfolding. Life circumstances and choices give form to this unfinished mold. An encouraging environment will nurture our natural talents and tendencies. Harsh environments may virtually wipe out our propensities; thus, we lose a vital part of ourselves and end up with confusion, dissatisfaction and low self-esteem. Or, difficult life experiences may challenge us to reach deep for traits we did not believe we had. While examining yourself, you may need to look past the appearance of your outer form back into that underlying core.

As the self grows, the characteristics which come more naturally develop first. Latent characteristics will then emerge as they become necessary to function in the world. Some natural tendencies are subdued by life situations in which parents, schools or other environmental influences do not encourage the basic core to unfold. For instance, Paula, who was imaginative and interested in arts, music and theater, was urged by her stepfather to take academics more seriously. Although Paula continued with her artistic interests during childhood, she sought other ways to achieve adult approval and minimized these interests as an adult. Maria showed natural tendencies for leadership in a nurturing and helping atmosphere. She enjoyed caring for children. These characteristics were channeled into raising her own family, and her leadership qualities did not continue to develop during her adult life. Thus, you may be reinforced for some of your tendencies but not have the opportunity to develop other sides of yourself.

Recognize the importance of developing all parts of yourself and don't become too one-sided. If you don't nurture or allow the weaker side to develop, it will emerge in a crude and incomplete form.

Recognizing this other side helps to keep you at an equilibrium. For instance, Maureen showed strength in leadership and organization. These traits brought her success and popularity at school and in her work life. Yet, being spontaneous and sensitive is unnatural for her, which has made it difficult for her to express herself in intimate relationships. To stay in balance, you need to rely on your strengths while you develop your weaknesses. Once you have developed all sides of yourself, you can ascend with a complete sense of self.

Acknowledging Your Masculine and Feminine Traits

EASTERN PHILOSOPHIES AND JUNGIAN theory separate the human psyche into masculine and feminine elements. The masculine side represents the active, outer-oriented, powerful, experiential and logical part of yourself, while the feminine represents the receptive, inner-oriented, harmonious, feeling and intuitive side. Traditionally, women are taught to express and develop their feminine qualities, and not to express and develop their masculine attributes. Whereas men are taught to develop and express their masculine traits, and not to develop and express their feminine qualities. Yet, men and women possess both. In order to feel more at ease in the world, to be true to yourself and to be whole, you must integrate your masculine and feminine sides.

Women use their feminine part to tune into other people's needs, to relate and to stay open. Their natural sense of harmony helps with balancing, reconciling and collaborating. Their intuitive nature aids in seeing the possibilities, explaining the unexplainable and conceiving the inconceivable. Women can also exercise their masculine part to initiate, analyze and achieve. In traditional worksettings, feminine qualities are not valued as are masculine ones. Hence, women often feel less than men. In these same settings, women who regularly use their masculine traits at work have been labeled "aggressive" or "cold." It may be that these women express primarily masculine traits, which to the observer may appear unsuitable for a woman because the observer inappropriately expects women only to possess feminine qualities. Yet the very same words may denote praise when describing a man.

It is eminent that all people bear their feminine characteristics into the world of work. Rationality, external power and physical dominance has brought progress and material abundance to our world but also many of our global problems, such as the unequal distribution of wealth, harmful "side effects" to the earth, and violent aggression. We must take heed of our softer feminine traits, which will engender a more humane world. We must become concerned with living creatures and serving other people's needs. Teachers today are cognizant that children need to be nurtured as well as taught. Teachers help children value themselves and others, express their feelings and cooperate and work together. Companies are also recognizing the value of serving people's needs because doing so creates happier and healthier employees, which generates greater productivity. In a grander view, companies could demonstrate the standard of "doing unto others as we want done unto us," which is urgently wanting in our world.

At the same time, we all must carry on masculine qualities such as initiative, risk-taking and vitality. These are the values of traditional American culture that brought about creative accomplishments and inventions in science, technology and the humanities. Both men and women must integrate their masculine and feminine sides; when this happens, humanity can evolve to the next level in which we continue to innovate, go out on a limb, do it, expand, and produce while being sensitive and aware, and tend to those around us. Instead of making decisions based on facts and logic alone, we can consider our values and the needs of other beings. Instead of only seeing what is concrete, material and pragmatic, we can strive to see the possible, unseen and ideal. In our emerging new world, both masculine qualities of "doing" and feminine traits of "being" will be revered.

Uncovering Worksettings You Like Best

EXAMINING PERSONALITY IS ALSO USEFUL in determining what type of work or what types of worksettings you prefer. In *Making Vocational Choices: A Theory of Vocational Personalities and Work Environments*, career theorist John L. Holland states that in order to be satisfied with your work you must choose an environment that fits your personality. People with similar personalities will cluster to particular worksettings. This is easy enough to envision. Think of the stereotypes for various occupations: the absent-minded professor, the fastidious accountant, the eccentric artist, the nurturing preschool teacher, the rugged construction worker, and the shrewd used-car salesperson. When you look at the overall fields, you will find many similarities among personalities. However, variations do exist within fields and within professions.

A Word about Personality Tests: Several personality inventories have been designed to help categorize interests and personal traits into classifications. Although no theory suggests that there is a limited number of personality types, they do suggest that individuals possess certain characteristics that are associated with particular types. Assessments help you uncover aspects of yourself of which you may not be aware or that may be puzzling. Instead of relying on outside feedback, take an honest look within and unveil how you see yourself. You may then choose the aid of a personality test in order to compare impressions.

Exercises

A. Fantasy Worksetting

To begin, use the relaxation narrative in the appendix.

Imagine yourself awakening on the morning of an ideal workday. Picture yourself getting ready for work. What time is it? What is your morning routine? With whom, if anyone, do you live? Imagine dressing for work. What type of clothing do you wear?

Now imagine yourself going to your place of work. How do you travel? What type of scenery do you pass? What is the climate like? Picture yourself arriving at work. At what type of location is it? Do you work indoors or outdoors?

Now approach the worksite. Picture what it is like. With whom, if anyone, do you work? Do you work together in collaboration? Do you give directions? Do you work alone? What is your relationship with your co-workers? What kinds of activities do you engage in? What kinds of tools or machines do you use?

You are an expert in your field and feel very good about your work and yourself. As a reward for performing well at your job, your boss or partner comes to you with four projects for you to complete. Any of the projects will take the same amount of time to perform and will offer the same amount of recognition. Use your imagination to fill in the details of these assignments. Here are the parameters of each assignment:

- In the first assignment, you will use your mind to think of an innovative plan, a new concept, or a solution to a problem.

- In the second assignment, you will use your physical strength or agility, specific tools or machines, and/or your knowledge of specific techniques.

- In the third assignment, you will use your interpersonal skills to work with others or to lead others toward a completed task.

- In the fourth assignment, you will complete your task by collecting, categorizing, or computing information or numbers for a report or summary.

Now choose which assignment you prefer to use in your fantasy work environment. Once you have decided, imagine specifically what work you would do to complete the assignment. When you are done with your fantasy, write down the details of the job you imagined and what skills you used to complete it. Consult Table 2, page 71, to examine your answers to this exercise.

B. Manifest the Real You

Picture yourself in your current or past job. List the characteristics from the exercises Describe Yourself and Uncover the Real You (in chapter two) that you express in this worksetting. Answer the following questions.

- Which traits that are stifled in this setting would you like to express?

- How would you go about expressing these traits?

- How would you go about expressing these characteristics in other areas of your life?

C. Your Masculine and Feminine Sides

Draw a line across a piece of paper. Label one end of the line "Masculine" and the other end "Feminine." Think of a very masculine person you know and admire, and list this person's traits under the "Masculine" side of your continuum. Next, think of a very feminine person you know and admire, and list this person's traits on the "Feminine" side of your continuum. Place an "X" at the point on the line that represents where you are between "Masculine" and "Feminine."

- Are you happy with where you are on the continuum? If not, what steps can you take to go in the direction you would like to go (toward masculine or feminine)?

59

- Can you think of times when you expressed masculine or feminine qualities more than usual? Describe these times.

- What specific masculine or feminine qualities would you like to have more of?

Profile: Paula Dombrowski

A. My Fantasy Worksetting

I'm brainstorming and creating with a partner. We make something from scratch. My beautiful surroundings make it easy to work. I work in a large, old house with lots of airy rooms. We work with pads, colors, fabric, and different tools and machines to create our product. I co-own a shop. We also run classes. I chose the first project, with the third as a close second.

B. Manifest the Real Me

When the children were home, I was happy because I could be involved with others in a creative and helpful manner. In my husband's business, I learned to be organized and meticulous, but I mostly enjoyed being hospitable and gracious. He didn't appreciate my creative changes. We have already come to a truce on this matter. It would be better to express my creativity in another setting. I have thought of taking classes, joining a theater group or the like. But, what about a career?

Paula (continued)

C. My Masculine and Feminine Sides

Feminine X	Masculine
Intuitive	Vital
Artistic	Takes initiative
Accommodating	Logical
Communicative	Decisive
Aesthetic	Competetive

I'd like to have more masculine qualities such as those I've listed above. I don't like being logical and decisive, but I feel that it would be useful in the business world. When I'm excited about an idea, I can be vital and take initiative.

Profile: Maureen Casey

A. Fantasy Worksetting

I'm in a plush office and use the phone often. I have a male secretary and a large staff who are very efficient because I hired them. I organize and I solve problems. I leave the workplace often to see clients. When I walk around, people recognize me and greet me, not only because they like me but because they respect my accomplishments. I'm in a service occupation where I insure satisfaction through my leadership of others and organizational ability. Part of my work is done outside. I prefer both the second and third assignments.

B. Manifest the Real Me

In my job I am: efficient, logical, decisive, practical, responsible, organized, and structured. I would like to speculate, be more influential, use more authority, lead, aspire. I can grow in my current field, I could change hotels, or I could start my own business.

Maureen (continued)

C. My Masculine and Feminine Sides

Masculine	X	Feminine
Physical		Expressive
Aspiring		Nurturing
Rigorous		Empathetic
Rational		Accepting
Pragmatic		Graceful

I would like to use more feminine qualities in my interpersonal relations. I sometimes feel unbalanced. I'd like to be more expressive, empathetic, accepting, and nurturing.

Profile: Maria Diego

A. My Fantasy Worksetting

People are busy working together toward a common goal. Although we have our own space, we usually spend time in each others' offices or in a meeting room. I feel the buzz of energy. I help people in need. I plan and organize and supervise others. I chose the third assignment, and the last as a second choice.

B. Manifest the Real Me

Traits I can express: Efficient, personable, responsible, tactful, thorough, orderly.

Traits or interests I would like to express: sociable, empathetic, cooperative, nurturing, more direct planning of services, helping people. I do some of these at work, but they are not the main purpose of my job. I was able to be more service-oriented when I was a receptionist. I currently have little contact with patients. To change this, I could train to become a nurse, or go back to a front-office job. If I had the time, I would volunteer to work with kids in need or trouble. Could I go to school to become a doctor?

Maria (continued)

C. My Masculine and Feminine Sides

Feminine	X	Masculine
Helpful		Technical
Collaborative		Assertive
Gracious		Thinking
Charitable		Determined
Feeling		Hands-On

I feel that I have qualities from both sides. There are some traits like technical and mechanical which I view as more masculine and believe I need. But I actually have these traits, using them in female settings; for instance, I fix all the broken things at home.

Profile: Sara Harris

A. Fantasy Worksetting

I work at home and alone. The crux of my work is writing about possibilities. I travel to do research. I converse with others over the phone. A couple of times a week, I go out and visit others who are involved in this project, and we discuss work over lunch or dinner. Or they come to my home for dinner and we work intensely all night putting ideas together. It's important that I merely need to come up with the ideas and spell them out. The actual working of the plan is taken over by others. I prefer the first project.

B. Manifest the Real Me

Characteristics I express in social work: altruism, empathy, influence, perception, and intuition. While doing research, I can be inquisitive, analytical, cognitive, and logical. The combination satisfies me a great deal. Yet why am I dissatisfied? I want more time to contemplate, to be more virtuous and devoted to my work, and to express more creativity and innovation. I want more autonomy. I enter every new project with these things, but they get lost in the process.

Sara (continued)

C. My Masculine and Feminine Sides

Feminine	X	Masculine
Altruistic		Analytical
Intuitive		Enterprising
Aesthetic		Goal-oriented
Process-oriented		Logical
Harmonious		Judicious

I prefer my feminine side but can show my masculine side. I think I have not always appreciated the possibilities and depth of the feminine side.

CHAPTER IV

Interests:
Discover What You Love to Do

Many interests are determined early in life. Before you began school, you preferred certain toys and activities over others. At school, you may have liked social studies or art classes and disliked math and gym. You preferred certain games over other games, some people over others, and certain movies, books, and rock bands over others. Some interests were encouraged and others were not.

Interests change as you encounter different ideas, milieu and influences. Exposure to a wide variety of subjects, environments, concepts and opportunities is important in selecting educational and career options. Opportunity and experimentation provide the basis for a positive developmental process. When encouraged, you have the opportunity to develop your interests. Some you continue to explore and cultivate, while others disappear. It's a shame when youthful interests are not cultivated due to wanting environments or squelching by others, yet it's never too late. Even as an adult, try to stay receptive and explore a great deal. Be sure to take a sound look at your interests before identifying your skills and abilities.

Why Your Dreams Are Important

IN THE PREVIOUS CHAPTER, YOU WERE asked to imagine a fantasy work environment. You may wonder how fantasizing will help you find a career. For most people, imagining and fantasizing has not been encouraged. In school, children are reprimanded for daydreaming and are told to get their heads out of the clouds. I advocate the opposite. Dream. Fantasize. Imagine. Desire. By connecting with this part of yourself and allowing it to thrive, you will sooner find a satisfying occupation than by testing your aptitudes. Your dreams are important. They don't appear by mistake. Your desires are clues from your inner self, indicating what you really want and who you really are. As we grow up, we are misled by who we think we should be, and in becoming that, we forget our dreams, fantasies and original desires. Ignoring your fantasies daunts them from appearing freely. Because we spend most of our time abandoning or downplaying our dreams, our inner selves become hesitant and covert about showing what we really want and need to do with our lives, sometimes to the point that we do not remember our fantasies at all.

Therefore, if you really want to fulfill your life, to do what is most meaningful to you, and to contribute something special and authentic, pay attention to your dreams. On the other hand, if you want a career that is practical and sensible, you don't need this book. You can either continue at what you are doing or seek a secure occupation which is in high demand. By being practical and sensible, you may find a job, but will you thrive in that job? If you have not freely fantasized about careers or your life dreams, try it and watch your inner horizons widen. Once you are clear about who you are and the interests you have, you can begin to analyze the practicality of pursuing these interests and fulfilling your fantasies.

Your Basic Interests

THE WORLD OF WORK IS DIVIDED INTO FOUR basic categories: data, people, things, and ideas.

Identifying your preference in these areas is the first step toward identifying your interests. Use the table below to examine your answers to the Fantasy Worksetting exercise from the previous chapter.

Table 2: Key to Fantasy Worksetting Exercise

First Assignment: If you chose this assignment, you prefer working with *Ideas*. Those who work with ideas use information and/or imagination to formulate thoughts, concepts, interpretations or plans. For instance, a scientist may have an idea for a hypothesis, a writer puts ideas into words, and a teacher assimilates and organizes ideas to present to students.

Second Assignment: If you chose this assignment, you prefer working with *Things*. Using things means using tools, such as scissors or a screwdriver; or machines, such as computers or a backhoe; or your hands or body, as in dancing or pottery. When you prefer working with things, using tools, machines or your body is the crux of your work.

Third Assignment: You prefer working with *People* if you chose this assignment. Working with people includes relating to people on all levels, such as taking orders and serving food, meeting together to complete a project, selling a product or service, or guiding others toward a career goal.

Fourth Assignment: If you chose this assignment, you prefer working with *Data*. Those who use data like to work with numbers, symbols, formulas, words and maps. An attorney investigates to obtain information to defend a client, an accountant records and computes numbers, and a typist organizes and types data.

Exercise

What's Your Preference?

Often you will use a combination of all four categories (people, data, things, and ideas) and will find it difficult to choose a preference. However, suppose you had to select a job that only involved one of the assignments: the use of machines and/or tools, processing information, speaking to or signaling people, or formulating ideas. Which would it be? What is your second choice? Third? Fourth? How does your choice compare with the assignment you chose in your Fantasy Worksetting?

Profile: Paula Dombrowski

What's My Preference?

People, ideas, things, data.

I chose the first assignment, which means I prefer working with ideas. My fantasy included people, ideas and things.

Profile: Maureen Casey

What's My Preference?

Things/people, data, ideas.

I chose the second and third assignments, which means I prefer things and people. My fantasy focused on people.

Profile: Maria Diego

What's My Preference?

People, data, ideas, things.

I chose the third assignment, which means I prefer working with people. My fantasy emphasized working with people.

Profile: Sara Harris

What's My Preference?

Ideas, people, data, things.

I chose the first project, which means I prefer working with people. My fantasy was to use my ideas.

CHAPTER V

Skills:
Inventory Your Experiences

The Question
of Aptitude

MANY PEOPLE CRINGE AT THE TERMS "skills" and "aptitude" and avoid thoroughly reviewing their skills. Much of their difficulty lies in the fear of not being "good enough." Yet, in seeking careers, individuals are quite concerned and preoccupied with their aptitude or skills. Most clients and students initially seek out my services to find out "what they are good at."

It's important that you have the potential to gain skills for a particular field. You must also be realistic about what you are capable of doing or of learning. More often than not, individuals undervalue their potential. They underestimate their skills because they had negative experiences with certain subjects in school or with school entirely, because they feel inadequate due to other life experiences, or because they fear failure. Hence, many people do not aspire to their potential.

75

If you do not possess the skills you need for a career, you can acquire these skills.

Skills can be learned in many ways: reading, observing, imitating, receiving on-the-job training, or taking apprenticeships or classes. Formal training is not the only method for obtaining skills. Those with deep commitment to achieving their dreams overcome obstacles for their quest through trial and error and much practice. The question of potential has a great deal to do with the willingness and commitment to obtaining the necessary skills.

It would be convenient to already possess all the skills necessary for your chosen profession. We all know individuals who excel in sports, are extremely organized and efficient, or are creative at making things without a recipe or pattern. This type of skill, which seems to come naturally, is called talent. Gifted people seem to effortlessly use their inborn skills. In reality, they have received the gift of discovering what they love to do. Because they enjoy what they do, they nurture their fancy by practicing and, in result, become more proficient. Everyone has a special skill or talent. Not everyone, however, recognizes or nurtures their gifts. We, our parents, our teachers, and so on, decide whether these talents are worth cultivating.

To cultivate skills, you need opportunity and nurturing. If, as a child, you had occasion to earn money, possessed a bank account, and had a female role model who made financial decisions, it would be normal for you to take charge of your money matters. If you had music lessons and enjoyed attending musicals and plays, in your adult life you could continue to participate in these activities or observe as a spectator. If your parents were schooled and valued education and encouraged you to take college preparatory courses in high school, you would most likely attend college.

Exposure creates the opportunity for obtaining skills. Determining your skills based on past opportunities alone is unfair to you and to the world. Paula, who wanted to become a fashion designer, heard that the fashion industry was extremely competitive. She did not pursue her interest any further than designing and making her own clothes because she didn't have a competitive edge. Sara thought she would enjoy the foreign service. When she learned that they required fluency in languages, she discarded her ambitions because she didn't do well in high school French. Parents and teachers, wanting to save children from failure, falter at supporting young people's dreams. Often women are not encouraged in school because "they are just girls and get married and have children, anyway." Maria, an excellent student in both math and the sciences, and who was interested in medicine, was not recommended to complete algebra or take physics and chemistry by her guidance counselor because she was not planning to attend college.

All Your Experiences Define Your Skills

PEOPLE NORMALLY SELECT NEW JOBS based on comparable past work experience and, consequently, often feel stuck doing the same type of work. You don't have to choose a career based on past experience alone, since you may be very good at things you don't enjoy. Employers sometimes overlook a prospective employee's potential because of a deficiency in her work history. Maria had trouble obtaining employment after being home with her children because she lacked "experience." You must overcome some of these self-imposed or externally imposed barriers, learn to identify your skills from all experiences in your life, and be able to describe these to potential employers. Therefore, do not discount job possibilities because you believe you lack employment experience. Instead, review other activities in your life for skills that may relate to your job objective. For instance, Maria is patient and thorough at explaining homework assignments to her children. Maureen can successfully arrange a large dinner party at the last minute. Can you identify the skills used in these activities?

In assessing your own skills, first consider your daily activities, hobbies, interests and accomplishments as a means for identifying your skills. Second, identify which skills you need for your career. Third, determine which of those skills you have, and discern which skills you need to acquire. And finally, determine how to acquire the skills you want to learn. As part of this process, consider the time and effort involved in learning new skills and whether or not you are willing to strive for mastering them. Remember: Not everyone starts at the same place.

Two Types of Skills

THE TRADITIONAL VIEW OF OCCUPATIONAL fields consisted of separate and distinct jobs which required specific work-content skills. A newer view of occupations emphasizes similar attributes among jobs as well as common bonds between different occupations. Although the structure of occupations may differ, many have similar functions. When you understand how your skills relate to the common job functions in various occupations, you will be more prepared to make changes from one field to another.

Technical: Skills that are pertinent to a particular job or job clusters are called technical or work-content skills. Some types of technical skills include knowledge of legal terminology, drafting, computer operating, street language, and flipping hamburgers. Some of these skills are acquired either from special courses at school or from previous work and life experiences. These skills may come easily, or some practice may be required.

Functional: Those skills that can be transferred from one job description to another or from one occupation to another are called functional or transferable skills. These are the foundational skills necessary for a wide range of jobs. For instance, teachers write lesson plans, department managers write reports, and attorneys write opening and closing statements. Waitresses organize their parties and service in order to make the dining process flow smoothly; supervisors organize work schedules or their subordinates' activities. Functional skills are usually expressed as verbs: coordinate, communicate, refer, and direct.

Homemakers reentering the workforce often don't believe they have job-related skills because they haven't worked outside the home. Career changers may think they do not have the appropriate skills for their new field of preference. Without these skills, they think that they cannot find a good job. The purpose of the Inventory Your Experiences exercise is to help you identify your skills from past experiences, whether from actual jobs or from other activities in your life. The result will be a list of your skills that are transferable to various jobs or job functions.

Exercises

A. Skills Checklist[1]

Circle the skills you like or would like to use in a job. Assume that you are competent at all these skills.

1. Assemble: Fit or join together parts in order to make or repair.

2. Illustrate: Draw, sketch, paint, photograph.

3. Brainstorm: Think of new ideas or possibilities.

4. Edit: Rewrite or correct written material for publication or presentation.

5. Build/Construct: Make clothing, furniture, structures, gadgets or other goods.

6. Organize: Develop and arrange programs and/or projects.

7. Synthesize: Integrate ideas and information into a whole new idea.

8. Drive: Operate vehicle or machine.

9. Hypothesize: Propose the basis of a theory or conclusion by reasoning.

10. Design: Conceive, create or form a plan for a project, program or product.

11. Forecast: Estimate or calculate in order to predict.

12. Intuit: Use insight, hunches and foresight.

13. Negotiate: Bargain and arbitrate toward an agreement.

14. Act as Liaison: Serve as a link between individuals or groups.

---

[1] Adapted from Berg, *Career Metamorphosis*, 79-81.

15. Use Body Coordination: Use body strength, balance and coordination.

16. Initiate: Exert influence for bringing about new directions.

17. Budget: Plan for cost and expenditure of money or resources.

18. Empathize: Listen, accept, understand and appreciate.

19. Classify: Categorize and systemize data or objects into classifications.

20. Teach: Inform, explain or demonstrate.

21. Create: Originate, produce or bring into being.

22. Supervise: Direct and review work of others.

23. Read for Information: Thoroughly review written resources.

24. Perform: Express in artistic or entertaining form to an audience.

25. Counsel: Listen with objectivity; guide and encourage personal growth.

26. Analyze: Investigate, inquire and examine the parts of a whole idea, event or thing.

27. Calculate/Compute: Use basic mathematics to compute quantities.

28. Tend Animals: Feed, shelter, breed, train or show animals.

29. Innovate: Change, modernize or initiate new ways of doing things.

30. Mediate: Resolve or settle conflicts or differences by acting as an intermediary.

31. Question: Inquire, probe, challenge, doubt upon.

32. Promote: Sell or popularize through media or special events.

33. Write: Compose written forms of communication as in letters, articles, ads, stories or lyrics.

34. Sell: Present a product to potential buyer and convince of its merits.

35. Draft: Draw up plans based on specific dimensions or specifications.

36. Provide Hospitality: Welcome, provide pleasure to visitors, guests or customers.

37. Collaborate: Work together in joint effort.

38. Cultivate Plants: Grow food, flowers, trees or other plants.

39. Problem Solve: Identify sources of a problem and offer a solution.

40. Visualize: Form a mental image of ideas and possibilities.

41. Maintain Records: Log, record, itemize, collate and tabulate data.

42. Use tools: Use tools to mend, repair, build or make objects or machines.

43. Invent: Originate a new idea or product through experimentation.

44. Treat: Heal and take care of patients or clients.

45. Motivate: Stimulate, provide incentive or incite.

46. Use hand coordination: Use hands skilfully.

47. Research: Perform scholarly or scientific inquiry, study and analysis.

48. Conceptualize: Form ideas or theories.

49. Delegate: Authorize others to take on tasks, assignments or workload.

50. Audit: Examine records for accuracy.

51. Work Outdoors: Work outdoors.

52. Compile: Gather information or material.

53. Operate Machinery: Use large or small machines to complete task.

54. Speak Publicly: Present point of view to an audience with intent to inform.

Table 3, page 85, arranges the above skills under the categories of data, people, things and ideas. Highlight the skills you circled in the checklist above. Where do you tend to cluster?

B. Inventory Your Experiences

A thorough method for identifying your skills is to describe your successful, rewarding, enjoyable ventures. Include classes, extra-curricular activities, volunteer work, previous and current employment, hobbies, special projects or interests. Only choose endeavors that you enjoy.

1. List five of your best experiences. Describe each event in detail. Consider the strengths you have that were necessary to be successful. Use verbs for describing action-oriented behavior. These are your skills.

2. Identify each technical skill by labeling it with a "T." Identify each functional skill by labeling it with an "F." Note that some skills are both technical and functional.

3. Refer again to Table 3, and circle those skills that you listed in this exercise. In which fields do your skills cluster? How does this compare with the results of the Skills Checklist exercise above?

C. Create a Fictitious Company

You have the opportunity develop and establish your own company. Give the company a name and determine in which department you will work.

- What type of company will it be?

- What are you are manufacturing or selling, or what service you are providing?

- What is your department's role in the firm?
- What are your responsibilities?
- What skills do you use?

D. Skills Evaluation

Refer to the Skills Checklist exercise and determine the following:

1. Assuming you have all the skills on the checklist, which ten do you prefer most?

2. Describe how you have used these skills.

3. Describe how would you go about improving these skills.

Table 3: Key to Skills Checklist[2]

DATA	IDEAS	PEOPLE	THINGS
			Hands-On
Organizing	*Creative*	*Helping*	*(Specific)*
4 - Edit	2 - Illustrate	14 - Act as Liaison	1 - Assemble
6 - Organize	3 - Brainstorm	16 - Initiate	2 - Illustrate
17 - Budget	10 - Design	18 - Empathize	5 - Build/Construct
19 - Classify	12 - Intuit	20 - Teach	8 - Drive
27 - Calculate/	21 - Create	25 - Counsel	19 - Classify
Compute	24 - Perform	30 - Mediate	35 - Draft
35 - Draft	29 - Innovate	36 - Provide Hospitality	52 - Compile
41 - Maintain	33 - Write	37 - Collaborate	
Records	40 - Visualize	44 - Treat	
50 - Audit	43 - Invent	45 - Motivate	
52 - Compile		54 - Speak Publicly	
			Hands-On
Intellectual		*Leading*	*(General)*
7 - Synthesize		13 - Negotiate	15 - Use Body
9 - Hypothesize		14 - Act as Liaison	Coordination
11 - Forecast		16 - Initiate	28 - Tend Animals
23 - Read for Information		20 - Teach	38 - Cultivate
26 - Analyze		22 - Supervise	Plants
31 - Question		30 - Mediate	42 - Use Tools
33 - Write		32 - Promote	46 - Use Hand
39 - Problem Solve		34 - Sell	Coordination
42 - Invent		37 - Collaborate	51 - Work Outdoors
47 - Research		45 - Motivate	53 - Operate
48 - Conceptualize		49 - Delegate	Machinery
		54 - Speak publicly	

---

[2] Adapted from Berg, *Career Metamorphosis*, 83-84.

Profile: Paula Dombrowski

A. Skills Checklist

I cluster under Ideas/creative, and, on a lesser scale, under People.

B. Inventory My Experiences

Design Clothing for Festive Occasions and Performances:

Keep up on fashion trends - T

Envision idea - F

Find appropriate fabric - TF

Draw or mix patterns - TF

Sew, fit and adjust outfit - T

Work with others to coordinate ideas and activities - F

Received Creativity Award in Talent Show:

Read music - T

Practice voice - T

Listen to music - F

Perform - F

Write songs - TF

Collaborate with musicians - F

Cleaned a Client's Closet:

Observe body type and proportions - T

Discuss client's preference for styles, color, etc. - FT

Convince to make some changes - F

Clean and organize closet by style, color, etc. - F

Show how to mix and match - FT

Shop - F

Negotiate and persuade to follow my idea - F

Paula (continued)

Technical: Knowledge of fabric, fashion trends, fashion design; pattern making; sewing; music (reading and writing); voice; play piano.

Functional: Practice singing; perform in front of audience; write music; locate things (research); keep up with trends (through research); negotiate for prices; provide information; help others; answer questions; keep records; organize; train and supervise others; budget money; order supplies; teach; persuade.

C. Fictitious Company

Company Name: PJ Designs

Design fabric and clothing for working women. Own shop with original clothing.

My Title: Designer

My Responsibilities: Create prototype designs for fabric; create design for patterns. Teach fabric design. Brainstorm and conceptualize one-of-a-kind fabric designs by client request. I visualize based on their description (or my own ideas) and then illustrate these by drawing and painting. I'm constantly innovating when things don't work as planned (which they never do). Provide hospitality and act as liaison: I provide excellent service and will refer clients elsewhere if I cannot meet their needs. I collaborate with clients and other designers, such as interior designers.

D. Skills Evaluation

1. Illustrate, brainstorm, design, create, innovate, visualize, conceptualize, act as liaison, collaborate, intuit, promote, draft, sell

Paula (continued)

2. *Illustrate:* clothing designs, Christmas cards, landscaping. *Brainstorm:* come up with ideas for costumes, banners, parties, decorating, vacation alternatives; help children solve problems. *Design:* clothing, costumes, furniture, draperies, various crafts, landscapes. *Innovate:* Improvise recipes, patterns (clothing, drapery), when camping or on vacation. *Visualize:* Remodel and redecorate homes, clothing, costumes, gardens. *Conceptualize:* All the above when reading, thinking or talking about them. *Provide Hospitality:* To children, husband's clients, friends at dinner parties or other festivities. *Act as Liaison:* between parents and school, children and adults. *Collaborate:* on school, sports and other children's projects; with family on home projects; with husband on work and social activities.

3. I am competent at these, but can I really use these skills for pay?

Profile: Maureen Casey

A. Skills Checklist

I cluster mostly under People/leading, then under Things/hands-on (general), Data/organizing, and Data/intellectual.

B. Inventory My Experiences

Was Promoted from Secretary to Manager:

> Supervise clerical staff - F

> Delegate work - F

> Interview, hire and train new employees - F

> Solve problems between departments - F

> Review work done - TF

> Run meetings - F

> Operate computer - TF

> Communicate with sales, restaurant, housekeeping and front-desk personnel - F

> Coordinate all arrangements for conference - F

> Troubleshoot - F

> Compile, organize, duplicate - F

Plan and Organize Holiday Party for 500 Employees:

> Plan details of event such as theme, food, people to invite, decoration - F

> Send out invitations, or call - F

> Organize preparation and activities - F

> Buy goodies - TF

> Order meals or snacks - TF

> Decorate in theme - F

> Socialize and make sure everyone enjoys self - F

Maureen (continued)

Took Trip to South America:

> Plan travel arrangements and basic itinerary - F
>
> Study maps, culture and language - FT
>
> Meet people from different places - F
>
> Try new foods - F
>
> Observe people, architecture, and natural beauty - F

Technical: Operate IBM and Apple PC using DOS and WordPerfect; gourmet cooking; protocol and etiquette; numerical skills; speak Spanish.

Functional: Organize activities, people, tasks, paperwork; plan events or tasks; locate, order and purchase items; negotiate prices; supervise, evaluate and train others; direct others.

C. Fictitious Company

Company Name: Outdoor Travels

Arrange travel tours for special groups. Specialize in trips to observe and enjoy natural beauty. (Outdoor and physical coordination).

Title: Owner

Responsibilities: Ascertain clients' interests; make contacts (*initiate*); arrange (*organize, negotiate, budget, mediate*) travel plans; obtain natural and historical information; plan tour; train, supervise and delegate staff; do tour.

D. Skills Evaluation

> 1. Organize, budget, negotiate, supervise, delegate, initiate, use body coordination, work outdoors, assemble, problem solve

Maureen (continued)

2. *Organize* activities, people and tasks in and out of job. *Budget* personal and work accounts. *Negotiate* with vendors at home and on job. *Supervise* and *delegate* assistant and secretary. *Initiate* ideas for traveling and other outings. *Solve problems* at work. *Use body coordination and assembling skills* in skiing, hiking, team sports and sailing. Do these activities *outside*.

3. Already competent.

Profile: Maria Diego

A. Skills Checklist

I mostly cluster under People/helping, then under Ideas/Data/intellectual.

B. Inventory My Experiences

Moved from Receptionist to Office Manager in Medical Clinic:

Detect when clients are nervous and help calm them down - F

Help clients - F

Provide information about payments, appointments and policies - TF

Keep precise records of treatment, lab work, and prescriptions - T

Organize files and paperwork - TF

Order medical supplies - TF

Negotiate with vendors - F

Budget moneys and pay bills - TF

Supervise receptionist staff - F

Train new employees - F

Plan Afterschool Cookies and Milk Sessions:

Prepare snacks - F

Observe and remember what types of cookies certain children prefer - F

Listen to children talk to each other - F

Detect (feel) when children are upset - F

Casually offer advice or suggestions - F

Build trust - F

Ask questions and show interest - F

Be open and receptive - F

Do fun activities - F

Maria (continued)

Raised $5,000 at Christmas Bazaar:

> Determine what to sell - F
>
> Make list of materials needed - F
>
> Find places that will donate or offer major discounts - F
>
> Organize and direct committees to help - F
>
> Find people to make or teach crafts - F
>
> Prepare mailing list - TF
>
> Make displays - FT
>
> Organize activities and games - F
>
> Organize staff and kids - F
>
> Solve problems as they arise - F
>
> Collect and count money - F

Technical: Medical terminology; numerical skills; sports knowledge (rules and regulations); operate computer, typewriter and copy machines; cleaning and mending; childcare; and diseases.

Functional: organize people and activities; make schedules; persuade people; teach children; help those with problems; communicate ideas; put people at ease; discipline and enforce rules; solve problems; buy goods; prepare items; decorate house.

C. Fictitious Company

Company Name: Our Children Cooperative Medical Service

Businesses and schools participate. Parents receive reduced care when they participate. Several doctors volunteer their time. I coordinate the program and also treat patients.

Maria (continued)

My position: I am a bilingual doctor. I listen and show compassion when people have problems (*empathize*). I *counsel* their emotional needs and *treat* their ills. I *act as a liaison* between patient, hospital or other medical agency. I *collaborate* with nurses, doctors and other medical staff. I *analyze* symptoms or test results. I *question* patients regarding symptoms and medical staff regarding results and diagnosis. I *research* when I'm unclear regarding an answer, treatment or diagnosis. I *problem solve* for different solutions.

D. Skills Evaluation

1. Empathize, counsel, provide hospitality, treat, act as liaison, collaborate, analyze, teach, question, problem solve.

2. *Empathize:* Listen and show compassion when people have problems. *Counsel* to their emotional needs. *Act as a liaison* between patient and doctor, hospital or other medical agency. *Collaborate* with nurses, doctors and other medical staff as in medical assisting. *Analyze* my own children's (or those of the children I'm watching) problems and offer solutions (*problem solve*). *Question* patients regarding symptoms. *Teach* children to do different things around house.

3. If I want to work in the medical field as a nurse or doctor, I will need the specialized medical training. However, I can gain hands-on skills on the job by observing, asking questions, or getting formalized training.

Profile: Sara Harris

A. Skills Checklist

I cluster under Ideas/creative and intellectual.

B. Inventory My Experiences

Direct KIDS FOR LIFE:

> Help others identify problems - F
>
> Help others find solutions to their problems - F
>
> Supervise paraprofessional staff - F
>
> Hire and train paraprofessional staff - F
>
> Create ideas for programs - FT
>
> Write reports, proposals - FT
>
> Budget moneys - TF
>
> Keep charts on all clients - TF
>
> Research field and new ideas - TF

Graduate School Research:

> Read books on topic - TF
>
> Develop own ideas - TF
>
> Develop hypothesis - TF
>
> Develop experimental design - T
>
> Collect data - TF
>
> Analyze data - TF
>
> Interpret results - TF
>
> Synthesize data - TF
>
> Write about results - F
>
> Present results to professors - F

Sara (continued)

Teach Class I Designed:

    Research topic - F

    Plan class: ideas for discussion, ideas for exercises, prepare examinations, prepare lectures - F

    Do class (lecture, discussion, examination) - F

    Read homework and exams - F

    Interact with students - F

    Recordkeeping/grading - T

Technical: Research; design; statistics; therapeutic methods; proposal writing; government budgets/procedures.

Functional: Research topics; analyze data and people; counsel people (listen, empathize, urge, analyze, suggest); solve problems; mentor others; write technical and creative works.

C. Fictitious Company

Company Name: Free School

School/college that emphasizes personal growth. Little delineation between faculty and students. No prescribed classes. People are there to learn and to help make this a better world.

My Position: Teacher. Design and teach classes as I learn about new topics of personal interest. I then can exhaust studies and teach others what I have learned. The enjoyment comes not only from giving but finding a new way to present information to others. These activities would include all of the skills in the next exercise.

Sara (continued)

D. Skills Evaluation

1. Brainstorm, intuit, create, design, synthesize, hypothesize, read for information, write, research, conceptualize, visualize, teach.

2. *Brainstorm* ideas for getting unmotivated clients/students interested. *Use intuition* with clients. *Design* programs, projects, class. *Synthesize* ideas when teaching, in research and writing. *Read for information* in research, grantwriting and for pleasure. *Write* papers, reports, thesis, journal, letters, stories. *Research* for papers, reports, grants, thesis. *Conceptualize and visualize* ideas based on conversation or research. *Teach* classes.

3. Improve intuition through trusting it more often, keeping track of dreams and other internal happenings, and meditating.

CHAPTER VI

Needs, Values, Roles: Understanding What Motivates You

At this point, you have accomplished the following:

- defined what type of person you are

- gained perspective on how you came to where you are in life

- explored worksettings you prefer

- uncovered the skills you like to use, those you feel comfortable using, and those you want to improve

Realizing your values is yet the most significant step in determining your life work. Values reveal your intentions and desires, such as the desire to be recognized, to help others or to express ideas. Values motivate you to become a famous singer or a good leader. They reflect lifestyle preferences such as living in a community and raising children or traveling the world and understanding other cultures. Values define your behavior, such as being cooperative, aggressive, fair, or intelligent. Values reveal universal views, as in desiring a world without war. Values impart what you find important at work, such as challenge, creativity and independence. Your values reveal the meaning and essence of your life as a whole.

How Needs Influence Values

THE PSYCHOLOGIST ABRAHAM MASLOW identified five basic human needs, beginning with physiological and ending with spiritual. One moves up the hierarchy as she fulfills the needs of the preceding level. The levels, in order of basic to more complex needs, are as follows:

- physiological, such as food and drink
- safety, such as shelter from harm and a comfortable environment
- love and belongingness, as in family and relationships
- self-esteem or acceptance for being oneself
- self-actualization, as in spiritual practices or philosophical questioning

Your needs influence which of your values will be prevalent. If you are hungry and cold, you value food and warmth. When you feel alone, you value companionship. If you are ill, you value health. In situations of need, people often value what they don't have or what is difficult to acquire. As circumstances change, values change. For instance, Maria moved from self-esteem to safety needs after her divorce and her values shifted from a need to express herself to those of financial security. As she made friends and gained confidence at work, she moved back up to love and belonging. Yet she still struggles with acceptance from her family. Maureen spent much of her adult life balancing her needs for belonging and sense of safety with occasional opportunities to fulfill her own self-esteem.

You can use Maslow's hierarchy in considering why the things you revere are important. Realize that your values will shift as a consequence of your circumstances. Review which of your needs have been met during your life and which of your values have remained prevalent. For instance, Maureen was raised with insecure financial circumstances and is resolute in striving for security. Maria grew up with a strong sense of family cooperation and harmony. Sara was rewarded for original thinking and individuality. Paula's sense of security and belonging came from being closely attached to her mother and later seeking approval from her stepfather.

Examining Your Values

CULTURE, ENVIRONMENT, AND FAMILY are other influences on your values. These along with individual needs can result in a unique combination of who you are and what you want from life. Which of these values stay with you and which are transitory? Which values that were passed on from your upbringing do you own as an adult? To answer these questions, look within and notice your shoulds and past influences.

At times, people become distracted from their innermost values because they are immersed in life's endeavors. People often are concerned with financial security, achievement and material comforts. In their quest for these things, they may lose the essence of what they are really striving toward. The prototype is the father who works long hours to provide for his family, yet does not have the time to spend with them. Working mothers may also fit this stereotype. Plainly, in a material world such as ours, financial security is important. It is significant, however, for us to examine the essence of what financial security provides.

Behavior: Values depict the standards of behavior or modes of conduct that individuals use in achieving their goals. For instance, both Maria and Sara want to help those in need. Maria, an extrovert and a helping type, prefers to have direct contact with those she is helping and see the results of her efforts. Sara, introverted and creative, would rather design projects or create materials to help society as a whole. Maureen is motivated to achieve her goals through competition, while Paula is inspired by collaboration.

Culture: Societies, cultures, countries, ethnic groups, religions, and political institutions influence values. Some cultures value elders because of their wisdom. The dominant culture in the United States, however, values youth; consequently, many people spend a great deal of effort and money to look, feel, and act young. Some cultures emphasize family or group loyalty. Traditional, western-American culture values rugged individualism. These values may diverge as the circumstances of society alter. If this country was attacked, people's values would change. Those people who grew up in the Depression have different values from those who came of age in the sixties.

In determining your values, you must sift through family, cultural and immediate influences and look underneath to find which values you intend to own. You may concur with your family's or culture's values or abandon some or all of these. With constant influence of family, friends, advertising, religion, and so on, it is difficult to identify what really is significant.

In the past, you may not consciously have contemplated your values in choosing a career. Now, in pondering these matters, you may feel impelled to acquiesce to certain values because you see no way of fulfilling others. How do you choose? What will be the consequences if you compromise? How do you know what you adopt now will be important to you later? When you look at what is most important to you at this time in your life, realize that your values may change as you develop or as your circumstances change. Yet, your core values remain with you throughout your life. These are the values you need to acknowledge in order to become whole and to express your inner being.

Table 4, a list of personal values, may help you identify your own values.[1]

---

[1] Berg, Astrid. "Fishing for Values." Values-clarification game. Capitola, California: SEFA Books, 1992.

Table 4: Personal Values

Adventure: Enjoying unusual experiences marked by excitement and suspense.

Aesthetics/Beauty: Being sensitive to qualities associated with truth, excellence, originality or harmony.

Altruism: Having unselfish concern for the welfare of others.

Charity: Acting or feeling with benevolence or good will.

Community: Enjoying the company of those living in my same locality and/or those with whom I have common interests or goals.

Cooperation: Working together toward a common goal for mutual benefit.

Creativity: Bringing about original and imaginative ideas or things.

Diversity: Appreciating variety and differences in life and lifestyles.

Economic Security: Being assured of financial security.

Education: Believing in the right to have an opportunity to learn through schooling.

Equality: Believing in equal opportunity for fellow human beings.

Faith/Hope: Having confidence in the future that is not dependent on logic or material evidence.

Fame: Attaining great recognition and public esteem.

Family: Having a close-knit family.

Financial Security: Being assured that I will always live comfortably.

Freedom/Liberty: Believing in the right to act how I choose and in political independence.

Friendship: Enjoying the company of those I like, trust, and receive support from.

Functionalism: Stressing practicality and usefulness.

Harmony: Being in agreement of feeling, action or approach with people or the environment.

Health: Living free from mental or physical disease or functioning.

Honesty: Practicing and appreciating truth, sincerity, honor and integrity.

Humor: Enjoying and expressing what is comical or funny.

Individuality: Being free from influence or control of others; asserting independence.

Interdependence: Being supported by, influenced by, and dependent upon another or others.

Justice: Practicing and honoring moral rightness, fairness, equity, and good reason.

Kindred/Kinship: Enjoying family or relations of common ancestry and character.

Knowledge : Being well-informed; continuing to learn.

Leisure: Enjoying freedom from time-consuming duties, responsibilities or activities; having free time to do what I want.

Table 4: Personal Values (continued)

Marriage/Relationship: Having a spouse, partner or friend with whom I have an intimate relationship.

Materialism: Desiring worldly possessions.

Mentor/Sage: Having the opportunity to teach and guide others, using my judgment, experience, and wisdom.

Moderation: Exercising self-restraint.

Nature/Environment: Respecting and caring for the physical world, including all living beings.

Peace of Mind: Having emotional and spiritual well-being; being content, calm, and serene.

Physical Fitness: Being physically fit, agile, coordinated, and having endurance.

Power/Authority: Having control and/or influence over others.

Prestige: Having prominence and influential status based on high achievement and character.

Prudence: Being wise in practical matters.

Public Welfare: Desiring health, happiness, and general well-being for all.

Self-confidence: Believing in my own abilities, goals and desires.

Self-understanding: Perceiving and comprehending my motives, feelings, thoughts, and behavior.

Spirituality/Religion: Following a philosophy, religion or path that emphasizes the spiritual rather than the material.

Success/Achievement: Attaining something desired, planned or attempted.

Technology: Applying science to industry and commercial uses.

Tradition: Following a set of customs or behavior that has been passed on from generation to generation.

Truth: Keeping to knowledge, fact, actuality and logic.

Way of Life: Having the opportunity to live the kind of lifestyle I choose.

Wealth: Owning a great quantity of valuable material possessions or resources.

Wisdom: Having good judgment; being informed.

Work: Enjoying physical or mental activity directed toward the production or accomplishment of something.

World Peace: Desiring the absence of war, quarrel, disagreement or hostility between states, nations, or peoples.

How Roles Affect Your Values

FOR MANY WOMEN, FAMILY TRANSCENDS the importance of a career. When women want both, they often feel guilty and are overwhelmed in the undertaking. As a result, they juggle schedules to attend baseball games and gymnastics competitions, make home-cooked meals, and participate in aerobics.

If you have a family, is it your role to cook, clean and be in charge of your family? Do you share these responsibilities with your spouse, or do you hire a housekeeper/nanny? If you share these roles, how are they divided between other family members? Both women and men must examine their roles. In most families, the woman does the "women's work" and men do "men's work." Therefore, in choosing work outside the home, women have a great deal to appraise because they are the managers of the families. Women's roles are typically tied to wifehood and motherhood (inside the home), and men's roles are tied to their work (outside the home). Family, generally, does not inhibit nor interrupt men's work as it does women at work. In deciding what you want from life and in determining your workstyle, you must appraise how to piece together your roles as mother, wife/partner, worker and person.

Women with wonderful families, successful careers and good relationships understand their values and preferences, have supportive mates, and have learned how to balance their work and family roles. A psychologist friend with three children has moved several times to follow her husband's career. His job possibilities were more restrictive than were hers. She works part-time and they both share childcare and household duties. Another friend had a successful service business. Her husband is in a management-level position in business. When they were ready to have children, she sold the partnership in her business in order to manage the home and family. These examples are characteristic of the way work, family and homemaker roles are being arranged. Although the numbers are growing, Mr. Moms are in the minority.

In assessing your values, look very closely at what traditional women's roles you choose to keep and which you do not accept.

Balancing Needs, Values and Roles

UNDERSTANDING WHAT IS *MOST* IMPORtant to you enhances your decision-making and goal-setting process. When your values conflict, attempt to create possibilities that will allow you to fulfill all your values. Richard Nelson Bolles, author of *What Color Is Your Parachute?*, said that we express ourselves in five realms:

- work

- relations

- leisure

- learning

- God

All of your values may not be attained solely in your career or solely in your personal life. Begin to think in terms of fulfilling your values both in your personal lifestyle and on your career path. While working several years in order to achieve the career recognition you value, you can also achieve, for instance, community/family values or creative values in your leisure activities and home life. Continued learning, service and spiritual undertakings may also serve values that are not attained at work. Act on your values in both work and personal life, and do not give up anything that is important. If you have neglected values that are now buried deep inside, dig them up. It's not healthy to ignore any aspects of yourself. Learn to balance your own needs and values with those of others with whom you live. Thus, your task is to rediscover your values and embrace their intent. To creatively define yourself is to not compromise yourself.

Motivators at Work

WHAT YOU VALUE IN YOUR PERSONAL LIFE will carry over to what you find important at work. Family and cultural influences together with needs affect the work you choose and how you do your work. Some people behave differently at work than at home. By examining this difference, you may uncover unrealized values. Ask yourself these questions:

- Am I expressing or behaving a certain way at work because I don't get to at home?

- Am I behaving a particular way at home because I don't get to at work?

- Am I seeking to achieve several kinds of goals and forms of expression through different avenues?

- Where am I most content?

- Do I want to integrate aspects of myself in different settings?

Your answers to these questions will help you find harmony between your work and home life, and within your workstyle. The Work Values Inventory exercise will also help you clarify what you want from a career.

Exercises

A. What Do You Desire?

To begin, use the relaxation technique in the appendix.

Imagine yourself walking along a familiar and comforting path. It's a warm day; you feel completely relaxed and you expect something special to happen during your walk. As you are strolling, you find an interesting item along the way. What you find represents something you value and desire. You pick up this article, study it, and store it somewhere on your person.

You continue walking and down the road find another item. The object seems as though it is calling you. You pick it up because it represents something that you value and desire. You find a place to put your second object to carry with you on your journey.

As you continue to walk, you find a third item that represents something you value and desire. You pick this up and find a place to store it.

You resume walking and see a fourth item that represents something your value and desire. Intrigued by this fourth item, you pick it up and find a place to store it.

You continue your walk, but begin to feel the burden of carrying so many things with you. You want to keep all four items and continue walking. You now discover a fifth article that catches your interest. You are drawn to pick up this article and carry it with you on your journey.

As you resume walking, you feel more and more burdened, and realize that you cannot carry all five objects. You must leave behind two of them. You stop and you stand a moment to decide which two items you will leave. This is a difficult decision because you truly value all five. You decide which three articles you will carry with you while you continue on the path, leave the two items behind, and resume your journey. Eventually you return home with your items.

When you are ready, open your eyes. Write down what your five objects were, what they represent, which ones you kept and why.

B. How Needs Influenced Your Values

Identify which levels of Maslow's hierarchy of needs you have experienced during the different stages in your life. Discuss how you ascended up and down the ladder of needs. Describe the values for each shift on the ladder. Where are you now? Why?

C. Owning Your Values

Make a list of values that are important to your family and/or your culture. Highlight the values you share with your family and/or culture. Are the values you highlighted really yours? Why are they important to you?

D. Determine Your Fulfilled and Unfulfilled Values

1. Get paper and different colored pens, pencils or highlighters. Sit down in a comfortable spot. Write down the things that are most important to you in life. As you are writing, pay attention to what you are feeling. When you have completed your list, review it. Is there anything you would like to add or delete from the list? Make these changes as needed.

2. With one color, highlight the items that are fulfilled at this time in your life.

3. With a different color pen, highlight those items that are not fulfilled at this time. (This will comprise the "Want List" mentioned in the next exercise.)

4. Write down what steps you need to take to attain the things you want in life.

E. Uncover the Essence of Your Desires

When you are done with the above exercise, rank your "Want List" (from #3 in Exercise D) and describe why these items are important to you. Describe the essence of each of these desires.

F. Evaluate Your Life Goals

Note: The following two exercises may be done as guided visualizations.

1. Think back on when you were a child or teenager. What were the things you expected to accomplish? What did you want to do? Whom did you want to become? What kinds of things were important to you? Make a list.

2. Pretend you are ninety-five years old and you have grandchildren, great-grandchildren or other young folk around you. They are gathered to listen to your life story. Without going through the details of your life or telling the whole story, emphasize what you believe were the most important experiences in your life. What are these things? Write them down.

G. Create Your Own Roles

1. Identify all the roles you play, e.g., mother, wife, friend, lover, sister, employee, consumer, student. Rank these roles according to the time you spend in each.

2. Choose the roles you prefer and wish to continue to play. Rank these roles.

H. Create Your Own Schedule

1. Make a schedule of your most typical week. Include time spent for work, leisure, household chores, entertainment, personal hygiene, school, personal time-out, etc.

2. Imagine an ideal week. Make a schedule for that desired week, including time for work, leisure and other significant activities.

I. Work Values Checklist[2]

1. From the list below, circle the values that are very important to you in a work environment.

2. Add any of your work values that are not described above.

3. Choose your top five work values and put them in rank order.

Working with Public: Being in regular contact with the public.

Achievement: Having the opportunity to develop my potential.

Variety: Performing diverse and changing tasks or duties.

Intellectual Stimulation: Doing work that requires independent thinking and continuous learning.

Recognition: Receiving appreciation and acknowledgment for my work.

Moral Agreement: Doing work that concurs with my morals and values.

Way of Life: Doing work that enables me to live the kind of lifestyle I choose.

Flextime: Working according to my own desired schedule.

Economic Security: Enjoying the assurance of financial security.

Excitement: Working with constant commotion and furor.

Field of Interest: Working in a specific field and use learned skills.

Altruism: Contributing to the welfare of others and/or to help society.

---

[2] Adapted from Berg, *Career Metamorphosis*, section on work values.

Precision Work: Doing work that requires attention to detail and exact specifications.

Structure: Doing a job with set procedures and methods for completion of tasks.

Associates: Enjoying co-workers and/or supervisors.

Independence: Determining direction and nature of work without conforming to guidelines.

Tranquility: Enjoying a quiet, calm and composed work environment.

Prestige: Enjoying renown on job or in the community.

Challenge: Performing frequent problem-solving and troubleshooting.

Working Alone: Completing work on my own with minimal contact with others.

Creativity: Creating or designing new things, events or ideas.

Aesthetics: Adding beauty to the world or work in pleasant surroundings.

Routine: Having a regular schedule, specific duties and consistency.

Locality: Living and working in a particular area/location.

Risk-Taking: Doing work that requires frequent risk-taking.

Physical Work: Doing work that requires bodily strength, agility and coordination.

High Economic Returns: Doing work that has the potential to pay substantially.

Quest for Knowledge: Searching for knowledge, information or truth.

Working Outdoors: Performing work outdoors.

Influence: Having the opportunity to change people's ideas, attitudes and opinions.

Authority: Being entitled to decide, control, supervise and implement.

Leadership: Having the opportunity to guide, influence and direct others at work.

Profile: Paula Dombrowski

A. What Do I Desire?

Item 1: Multi-colored, tie-dyed bandanna, like something from the sixties but with more vibrant colors. Represents my desire to create and work with color.

Item 2: A mirror. Represents looking deeper into myself.

Item 3: A family photograph. Family.

Item 4: A tortoise. Patience.

Item 5: A golfball. Time with husband.

I keep items 1, 2 and 5 because I want to express my creativity; I need to look closely at myself ; and, having been so preoccupied with children, I desire more time with my husband.

B. How Needs Influenced My Values

I had all the things I needed as a child. I lacked self-confidence in grade school. I was a people pleaser (belongingness). By high school, I came out of my shell. I made costumes for the high school plays and sometimes had parts. I enjoyed the freedom of running a home over the confines of a nine to five job. I have had opportunity to do artistic projects for the children, our home and for myself. For instance, I sang in our church choir and performed at weddings (self-esteem). But now that the children are gone, and I have fewer responsibilities at home. I am bored. I read that boredom means you no longer want to do the things you can do (belongingness, esteem). That describes me now.

C. Owning My Values

Parents': Thriftiness, hard work, *family*, prudence, *financial security*.

For many years I tried to live up to those values. I realized that their needs were influenced by the Great Depression.

114

Paula (continued)

D. Determine My Fulfilled and Unfulfilled Values

Fulfilled:

>   good marriage and relationship with kids

>   financial security

>   good friends

>   successful and happy children

Unfulfilled:

>   Express creativity: I would like to take a class in fabric
>   painting or water color. I would like my own studio.

E. Uncover the Essence of My Desires

I have always discounted my creative desires and channeled this energy into my children's projects (for instance, making costumes for a play). It's important to me to do a creative activity or project for myself. By taking a class or finding space in my home for a studio, I will be acknowledging my creative self.

F. Evaluate My Life Goals

At 20: happy/healthy marriage and family; financial security; my own dress shop.

Reflections at 95: friends and family; expressing your true self; harmony; enjoying day to day; appreciating the small things; creating beauty.

G. Create My Life Goals

Current: Wife (confidant, secretary); homemaker; mother; artist; entertainer.

Preferred: Artist; wife (partner, confidant); mother (confidant); entertainer; mother (mentor).

Paula (continued)

H. Create My Own Schedule

Typical:

Weekdays

    7-8: dress/breakfast

    8-10: clean

    10-1: run errands

    1-2: lunch

    2-5: TV/shopping/visiting

    5-7: dinner

    7-10: TV

Weekends: No structure, garden, shop, recreate, socialize

Ideal:

Weekdays

    7-10 exercise/dress/breakfast

    10-11 calls

    11-3 creative work

    3-4 errands or home

    4-8 cook/husband/friends/dinner

    8-10 work or relax

    10-11 relax

Three-day weekend: No structure, family/friends, entertain, recreate

I. Work Values Checklist

    1. Creativity

    2. Aesthetics

    3. Economic Security

    4. Associates

    5. Independence

Profile: Maureen Casey

A. What Do I Desire?

Item 1: Valuable coin: Money earned and saved increases in value.

Item 2: Saw an eagle fly overhead: Leadership and influence.

Item 3: A key to success (at work). May also represent key to city. I want to have important role in my community or in an organization.

Item 4: Mother's Day Card: Success in raising children.

Item 5: A poker chip: Take a risk.

I kept items 1, 2, 3 because, since I live alone, I value financial security and want to live comfortably as I get older. I have leadership ambitions and I want an important role in my community. I already have good kids, and I'm not sure I'm ready for a big risk.

B. How Needs Influenced My Values

Belonging: I felt out of place at the new school I attended after my family moved to a bigger house in a more expensive neighborhood. I didn't dress right and my parents didn't own two cars. As an adult, when my marriage fell apart, I lacked a sense of belonging. As a single parent, financial security was important, but not so much to jeopardize time with my kids. Much of my esteem comes out of my success as a single mother, and now the accomplishments of my children. Love and belonging not only come from family but also from my social groups and at work. I get esteem from my accomplishments at work. I bridled some of these urges when the children were young. Now that they are nearly on their own, I am ready to "go for it." I'm seeking self-esteem and self-actualization.

Maureen (continued)

C. Owning My Values

Marriage/family; financial security; health; prestige; achievement.

I value all of these. It seems that my parents could not live up to their values.

D. Determine My Fulfilled and Unfulfilled Values

Fulfilled:

> happy and healthy kids
>
> financial security
>
> self-confidence

Unfulfilled:

> prestige (would like recognition in community or work; would like to be a leader. How? Take on more responsibility. Express my opinions and implement my ideas.)
>
> independence (start my own business)

E. Uncover the Essence of My Desires

1. My own business: Work that satisfies, provides good income, prestige and independence.

2. Large house with ocean view: comfortable, even luxurious lifestyle.

3. Money to send children to good college: Good education for children that would lead to comfortable and easier life than mine.

4. Success at work: Feel accomplished and challenged.

Maureen (continued)

F. Evaluate My Life Goals

As Youngster: Marriage/family; successful career; financial security; prestige; leadership.

95 Years Old: Self-confidence; fairness; stick to your goals; family.

G. Create My Own Roles

Current: Employee (organizer, listener, liaison); mother (cook, listener, adviser); own person (consumer, recreater); friend; mate.

Preferred: Business owner (organizer, initiator, liaison); own person; friend; mate; outdoors person; mother-listener/advisor; cook.

H. Create My Own Schedule

Typical:

    Weekdays

        6-7: prep for work

        7-8: drive

        8-12: phone calls, organize, troubleshoot, delegate, etc.

        12-1 if I'm lucky: lunch; work out 3x/week

        1-6: same as 8-12

        6-7: drive

        7-10: dinner, relax or work

    Weekends: Outdoors, entertain, work

Ideal:

    Weekdays

        6-7: work out

        7-8: prep for work

        8-10: phone calls, troubleshoot

        10-12: paperwork

        12-2 lunch/meeting

        2-5: miscellaneous

        5-10: relax, dinner, visit, entertain

    Weekends: Outdoors, entertain

Maureen (continued)

I. Work Values Checklist

1. Independence

2. Achievement

3. Leadership

4. Economic Returns

5. Prestige

Profile: Maria Diego

A. What Do I Desire?

Item 1: A child's drawing of family: Family.

Item 2: Something whittled: Look to the core.

Item 3: A Native American relic: Tradition.

Item 4: An abandoned doll: Help the children of the world.

Item 5: A book: Education.

I keep items 1, 4 and 5 because I love/value my family. I really want to make a difference in the world and help others. I would like an education. These are my most important desires.

B. How Needs Influenced My Values

During childhood, I alternated between security and belonging. I was different from other children in my neighborhood because I had a mother who worked. When my marriage was failing, I went from self-esteem to belonging and to safety when we divorced. Since security for the children was primary, I needed a secure job with medical insurance. After establishing myself in my work and I knew I could take care of my children's needs, I sought recognition from my parents, who still do not approve of my divorce. As I realize that they will not change, I now seek recognition in other areas of my life. I am now between belongingness and esteem. My self-image is changing, and service to others is becoming more important.

C. Owning My Values

Marriage/Family, community, tradition, *religion*, respect (for elders).

This is exactly what I am struggling with. I agree with these values; I just interpret them differently.

Maria (continued)

D. Determine My Fulfilled and Unfulfilled Values

Fulfilled:

> happy family
>
> good health
>
> family tradition

Unfulfilled:

> family: I feel responsible for the fact that the children do not have father around.
>
> help others: I would like to help mothers or children of single parents. Volunteer?
>
> financial security: Go back to school and get a better paying job.

E. Uncover the Essence of My Desires

1. Want my children to feel secure and loved. Do not feel that I can provide all to them.

2. Want to be more useful to others in need.

3. Want to feel financially secure. Don't want to worry about providing for children and myself.

4. Don't want to feel guilty for my marriage breaking up.

F. Evaluate My Life Goals

During Youth: Nice house; happy family; good-looking and providing husband; several friends.

95-year-old wisdom: Gratitude; enjoy close ones in your life; be giving to others; listen and watch your elders; always forgive.

Maria (continued)

G. Create My Own Roles

Current: Mother; employee; volunteer; friend; daughter.

Preferred: Mother; helper (work); organizer (work); wife; friend; teacher.

H. Create My Own Schedule

Typical:

> Weekdays
>> 6:30-8: morning prep
>> 8-12: work
>> 12-1: lunch
>> 1-5: work
>> 5-6: errands
>> 6-7: dinner
>> 7-9: kids
>> 9-10: relax, if I'm lucky
>
> Weekends: Shop, family, relax

Ideal:

> Weekdays
>> 6:30-8: morning prep
>> 8-12: work
>> 12-1: lunch
>> 1-3: work
>> 3-5: children
>> 5-7: dinner
>> 7-10: family/personal/husband
>
> Weekends: Time for family/friends

Maria (continued)

I. Work Values Checklist

  1. Field of Interest

  2. Altruism

  3. Associates

  4. Economic Security

  5. Leadership

Profile: Sara Harris

A. What Do I Desire?

Item One: A discarded fortune that said, "Don't let your ego keep you from taking a chance on your dreams."

Item Two: A little girl picking flowers for her mother. Represents yearning for motherhood.

Item Three: A white rock weathered to a perfect smooth roundness. Represents how life experiences mold us to perfection.

Item Four: A bird watcher. We converse and discuss why we enjoy this particular path. Represents desire to meet someone who walks a similar path, yet for a slightly different reason.

Item Five: A delicate flower that has been crushed. Represents my desire for growth.

I keep the rock, the image of the girl and the fortune. I actually once opened a fortune cookie that said I realize how important it is to follow my dreams. I very much want a child. I believe and value that all my experiences have meaning.

B. How Needs Influenced My Values

All needs up to self-esteem were met as a youth. As a teen, I didn't fit into the usual high school and college "social system." Seeking esteem and self-actualization has been my life dissension. I need to be independent, creative and flexible in life and in work. Security is not important in a physical manner. I seek emotional security which comes out of belonging. Where am I now? I am at a transition period. Where do I go from here with my life? I have achieved and been recognized professionally. Is that enough? Or do I need to fulfill a role that has been neglected?

Sara (continued)

C. Owning My Values

Education; self-expression; prestige; marriage/*family?*

I want to do what I want because I want, not because of how good it looks. I am unclear where family and marriage fits in my life. I am more interested in intellectual stimulation than education per se.

D. Determine My Fulfilled and Unfulfilled Values

Fulfilled:

> continued learning

Unfulfilled:

> creativity

> wisdom

> children

> inner peace

I am reaching for the stars. The things I want take a lifetime or many lifetimes to achieve. I could be doing more creative rather than intellectual pursuits in my work. Sometimes these pursuits oppose each other. To be creative takes more risking. How do I resolve my desire for children without a mate?

E. Uncover the Essence of My Desires

1. Child(ren): Love, teach, nurture, give, admire.

2. Self-understanding: To come to understanding.

3. New job: Independence and creativity.

4. Life mate: Someone to share my life with; intimacy, a partner, companionship, collaborating.

5. To travel and/or live abroad: Excitement, adventure, knowledge, sharing.

Sara (continued)

F. Evaluate My Life Goals

Early Expectancies: Save the world; live in community with many friends who share similar life goals; see major changes in education and welfare of those in need.

95 Years Old: Change the world by changing within. The greatest gift is love. Follow your heart not your mind.

G. Create My Own Roles

Current: Researcher; formal student; friend; writer; creator.

Preferred: Writer/creator; mother; partner/friend; informal student.

H. Create My Own Schedule

Typical:

Weekdays
8-10: yoga/meditate
10-12: phone calls/errands
12-3: write/research
5-7: dinner
7-10: work

Weekends: Some work, some play

Ideal:

Weekdays
8-10: breakfast with family, begin day
10-3: write/read (some days will be visiting friends for lunch, doing errands, etc.)
3-4: meditate
4-7: family/friends/dinner
7-9: counsel; or
7-11: family/friends

Weekends: Many trips to the country or city; see art; hear music, theater; go on picnics, bike rides; read by the fire; see friends

Sara (continued)

I. Work Values Checklist

    1. Altruism

    2. Creativity

    3. Independence

    4. Intellectual Stimulation

    5. Way of Life

CHAPTER VII

Creating Your Life Path: Combining Personality, Interests, Skills and Values

**Finding
Personal
Balance**

YOU HAVE REVIEWED YOUR LIFE HISTORY, analyzed and discovered who you are, identified your strengths and weaknesses, and clarified your values. The exercises in the preceding chapters have helped to elucidate who you are and to guide you toward your preferred worksettings and lifestyles. You may, however, still feel quite vague about what you want to do. You may have several new options you'd like to consider; or you may feel affirmed in ideas you had before reading this book. You may be overwhelmed by the reams of paper you've written during this process. You may be asking yourself, "What will I do with all this information? I'm confused about where to go with my life and how to get there." Streamlining this information is a multifarious process. The challenge is to realize all aspects of yourself. This process could take several months. The steps for integrating your history, personality, interests, skills and values are:

- Review your answers to the exercises in previous chapters and determine whether you have been honest in describing yourself and whether you have left out any pieces or information. Make any necessary changes or additions.

- Clue into the areas that need more attention or help restore balance in your life. Which parts of you are fulfilled and which are not fulfilled?

- Remove yourself from analyzing the information; let your intuition take over.

- Ask a trusted, objective and supportive friend to listen to you as you describe your values, interests, personality and skills. Ask the person to help integrate, brainstorm and support your inner self.

When you begin integrating the results of the exercises, you will find that they are not so precise as to confine you to one particular job; however, they are focused enough to envision a general environment, confirm the skills you like to use, and incorporate some basic work values. With your ideal job description, you can explore occupational clusters or specific occupations that interest you. You can match your personalized description to those of existing occupations and discern how closely these jobs fit.

On another level, you must continue to introspect and consult your intuition for information. Although your passions, history, inhibitions, doubts and visions may be clear to others, you must work these out in your own time. You must decide what you are willing to give up (compromise), what adjustments you will make, and how you can best fit your career needs to your personal life.

The following three exercises will help you uncover your career interests. The first exercise, Summarize Who You Are, asks you to review the assignments in preceding chapters, then do some exercises to help you integrate your personality, interests, skills and values. The purpose is to begin to develop harmony in your life. The second exercise, Getting to the Heart, encourages right-brain thinking. Review your notes in a detached manner and intuit work or life scenes, feelings, and career titles. Sifting through the information in this manner helps your inner self recognize your life mission and find your own truth. How to include help and ideas from others is described in the third exercise, What Does Your Coach Say? Outsiders can perceive the subtleties of your confusion and help you see beyond your fears and doubts.

Exercises

A. Summarize Who You Are

1. Summarize your personality characteristics and how you would like to express them in various settings, e.g. work, leisure, volunteer, family.

2. Describe the lifestyle and workstyle necessary to fulfill your personal and work values.

3. List the skills you would like to possess and how you would like to use these skills. Is your focus on data, people, things or ideas?

4. List the skills you need to improve. How will you go about improving these skills?

5. Based on the above information, write an ideal job description. Include duties, accountability, materials and equipment you would use and people you might work with.

6. List non-work activities important for you to express your holistic self.

B. Getting to the Heart

1. To successfully complete this exercise, you must be comfortable with yourself and the process. Make sure you are well-rested and that you are not preoccupied with problems, whether or not they relate to the topic at hand. If you use any meditative-like techniques to quiet your mind, do so before beginning this exercise. Other techniques to enhance this process may include exercising or engaging in creative outlets or something you enjoy that relaxes, comforts and pleases you.

2. Review your answers to the Exercise A as if you were reading another person's notes. Observe your thoughts and feelings that come up as you read.

Now find a mood, an essence, a quality, a symbol that reflects the descriptions you read. Do not force an answer. Do not reason or analyze. Use your intuition and imagination by, for instance, drawing a picture, writing a poem, or beginning to move, dance or perform. While rereading your summary, be aware of the following and write down all your reactions:

- What images, feelings or perceptions appear?

- What aspects of the summary create excitement?

- What effects strong emotions?

- When do fears and doubts arise?

- When are you blocked by shoulds?

C. What Does Your Coach Say?

In choosing someone for this exercise, make sure your listener can be objective and supportive. Invite your coach to read your summary in Exercise A. Ask the person for initial, intuitive impressions. You may also ask your coach to read the instructions of Getting to the Heart. After your coach is satisfied with expressing her right-brain ideas, ask if she has any analytical and logical responses. As a listener, do not dispute the responses of your coach. Merely write down her answers.

Profile: Paula Dombrowski

A. Summarize Who I Am

1. Personality Characteristics: Creative, imaginative, expressive, extravagant, non-conforming, idealistic, gracious, collaborative, communicative, aesthetic. I need an outlet for my creative self. I could take up a serious hobby and choose a people-oriented job. I'd rather try my hand at combining creativity and working with people.

2. Values: Marriage/children, creativity, aesthetics, associates, independence, self-confidence, economic security. To fulfill these in my lifestyle and workstyle: Live and/or work in beautiful, even extravagant surroundings. Work with people I like. Create beautiful things.

3. People/Ideas: Illustrate, intuit, create, promote, draft, sell, collaborate, visualize, innovate, design, conceptualize, brainstorm.

4. Need to improve negotiating, promoting and selling skills. How? Get a customer service or sales job. Sell my own creations. Get advice from people who have these skills.

Paula (continued)

5. Create objects of beauty. Bring others together to work on projects. Together with partner, formulate basic design incorporating materials, cost, time to complete, etc. Present to client and make changes where necessary. Design creative product or service for client with apparel problems/needs. Work in large and lighted studio with long worktables, drawing board, pencils and colored pens or paint, rulers, etc. Need sewing machines, mannequins, fabric, sitting area for guests, dressing room, tape measure, record/appointment book, swatches of fabric, several fashion magazines.

6. Need to balance the creating (which is quiet and concentrated work) with people contact. Could see myself working a people job in a creative environment. Or, I could break up my day in order to fulfill both needs.

B. Getting to the Heart

While I was painting with water colors, I produced abstract pieces with vibrant and bold colors (need to express). Inspired, I continued to work for several afternoons. Over time, my pieces began to take form, but remained vibrant. I felt inspired, angry and depressed. I'm still painting.

C. What Does My Coach Say?

Keep painting. Take my time to decide. Express myself.

Profile: Maureen Casey

A. Summarize Who I Am

1. Personality Characteristics: Efficient, logical, hospitable, pragmatic, organized, aspiring, dominant, persuasive, controlled, earthy, physical. I express all of these at work except being persuasive and physical. I could move up in the company and be more influential. I could start a business, which would include influencing others and being physically active.

2. Values: Self-confidence, health, family, power, independence, achievement, high economic returns, and economic security. To fulfill these in my lifestyle and workstyle: Continue the lifestyle I have formed over the years in which work is important but does not interfere with leisure time and family (although family is less important now). I'd be willing to give up leisure temporarily in order to start my own business. I want to be financially comfortable, be able to travel, and have time to pursue outdoor hobbies. In committing to a relationship, I will not lose my self-confidence and independence. I want to pursue career goals, whether through higher-level management (power to make decisions and determine my own work) or starting my own business. My workstyle is pretty driven, people-oriented, yet casual.

3. People/Things: Work outdoors, organize, use body coordination, initiate, provide hospitality, use hand coordination, problem solve, delegate, budget, negotiate

Maureen (continued)

4. Skills to improve: knowledge of starting a business, of traveling, of marketing/advertising, of accounting/bookkeeping. I can do this by reading or taking college courses.

5a. Indoor: Coordinate with organizations to organize and set up trip. Plan procedures and itinerary. Oversee details and arrange with staff and other agencies. Check for problems and details. Frequently communicate and travel to meet with clients. Provide exciting yet comfortable outings for corporate personnel in outdoors. Includes planning lodging, meals, outdoor excursions. Guests have a pleasant and enjoyable visit. Work in office with area for receiving guests. Need telephone, computer, car, office equipment (such as copy machine, fax), outdoor staff and hiking/skiing/scuba, etc., equipment.

5b. Outdoor: If I organized and led outward-bound survival or pleasure trips for executives, I could have the best of both worlds. If not, I would keep the business management oriented portion as work, and do my own trips for pleasure.

6. Outdoor activities such as hiking, camping, horseback riding, skiing, and frequent traveling.

B. Getting to the Heart

After a vigorous walk, I saw a clear image of myself running a business. I felt assured and powerful. When I began to think of the details, I could feel my body get tight. My doubts are around coordinating and balancing my personal life and work goals.

C. What Does My Coach Say?

My coach saw Robert, my fiance, as a partner. She suggested a clear division between work, home and personal time.

Profile: Maria Diego

A. Summarize Who I Am

1. Personality Characteristics: Personable, efficient, traditional, collaborative, serving, influential, altruistic, aspiring. Am efficient, personable, conforming and serving at work. Would like to empathize, influence, collaborate, and aspire. I don't think I have the energy to do this as a volunteer after working all day. I want this in a job!

2. Values: Marriage/family, faith, health, economic security, field of interest, altruism, associates, tradition. To fulfill these values in my lifestyle and workstyle: Family comes first. Work must revolve around family life. I want to help others, enjoy and collaborate with co-workers and have security. May do early shift in as hospital nurse, or work in a clinic.

3. People: Treat, counsel, act as liaison, mediate, provide hospitality, collaborate, teach, motivate, question, problem solve.

4. Need to improve treating, teaching, counseling, mediating and motivating skills. Can improve by taking courses in counseling, psychology and communication, and by volunteering in service work. Need to attend school to get treating/nursing skills.

5. Communicate directly with those in need. Provide comfort. Work closely with team toward common goal. Follow basic procedures to help others. Work closely with others in order to help, teach or treat. Meet with co-workers on regular basis, discussing individuals needs. Hospital or classroom.

Maria (continued)

6. Aside from time for family, I need to know I'm making an impact on others. I need direct people contact. I will think about going back to school to train for a job in medicine, education or social service.

B. Getting to the Heart

I envision Dolores Huerta and Marta Bernal. These women represent courage, altruism and service. I see dark eyes of children who smile in spite of their suffering. I was filled with emotion, and I had to stop the exercise. I wish I had the power to help.

C. What Does My Coach Say?

Go to school.

Profile: Sara Harris

A. Summarize Who I Am

1. Personality Characteristics: Empathetic, intuitive, non-conformist, cognitive, introspective, visionary, aesthetic, intellectual, creative. I can express most of these as a therapist. I'd like more opportunity to create and use my visions. Part-time counseling and part-time work in a creative field would be a good balance.

2. Values: Spirituality, creativity, independence, family, wisdom, intellectual stimulation, altruism, equality, way of life, continued learning. To fulfill these values in my lifestyle and workstyle: work at home with lots of time, freedom and opportunity to be creative. Choose my own projects that involve ideas, research, and writing and that will serve to help others. Live with people who share ideals.

3. Ideas: Brainstorm, synthesize, use intuition, teach, create, read for information, research, write, conceptualize, visualize, design, hypothesize, illustrate.

4. Skills to improve: writing through practicing and joining a writer's group.

5. Create and develop educational materials. Research current resources. Determine educational needs and brainstorm ideas to innovate resources. Provide stimulating and original programs, exercises and literature. Equipment would include: computer, personal library, desk, telephone, (fax?).

Sara (continued)

---

6. If I pursued a cognitive job and used intellectual/
   research-type skills on a part-time basis, I would
   need time to do creative work on my own time.
   This hasn't worked for me, so far. My own needs
   are placed on the back burner. I could work fewer
   hours and discipline myself to take time for creative
   outlets.

B. Getting to the Heart

Saw an image of an eccentric old woman. She lives in a wooded
area and is wearing colorful, flowing clothes. She's a mentor, or
leader to many, but spends much time alone. This is me in the
future.

C. What Does My Coach Say?

My coach asked me what I would do if I could complete any
project I've begun or start something new—without restrictions,
shoulds or guilt. My answer was I would put together ideas I have
for a workbook/workshop and test it on people with very
different backgrounds. She then asked, "What's stopping you?"

Part Three

Taking Action

CHAPTER VIII

Researching Career Opportunities

**Exploring
Career
Options**

NOW THAT YOU HAVE FOUND CLARITY about what you seek in a vocation, it's time to explore career options. As you have done in the self-exploration process, be sure you give yourself time to thoroughly explore and widen your horizons. The more you know about the world of work, the better choice you can make. First, seek basic information on occupations, companies and labor market trends. When you are ready for specific information, talk to someone who is already in the field you are considering.

Sources of Career Information: Table 5, found on page 149, lists the names of books, tapes, and software to aid in your research of possible careers. College institutions have career centers with information in books, on microfiche, on computers, and on audio- or videotapes. Public libraries also carry these resources. Several

145

systems exist for categorizing occupations, which can make it confusing for the novice. Allow yourself ample time to browse. Don't expect to find all the data you need on your lunch hour. Normally, resources are located in a reference section; thus you will not be allowed to take them home. Begin your search by seeking material on general occupational areas. If materials don't offer information on your particular field of interest, look for a related field or occupation. Most occupational guides offer general data that is based on national trends. Often the data is a bit outdated. Therefore, read the newspaper or publications in your field of interest for information on local salaries and trends.

Audio/visual sources provide more personalized information on occupations. For instance, job biographies are taped interviews with people about their jobs. Computer resources often combine career information with college information. The advantage of computerized information is the printout you receive to take home and review at your leisure. Use a combination of these resources to suit your needs.

Networking: People use friends, acquaintances, or anyone they know for information about occupations, educational opportunities, and jobs. This form of passing on information, called networking, is making use of your people contacts. It is advertising through word of mouth. When you need a mechanic or an orthodontist, you ask friends and acquaintances for recommendations. If you don't know someone in the career you want to explore, ask acquaintances, colleagues, classmates, friends, or relatives if they do. Most people are happy to share with you what they know or who they know. Networking is helping one another. Don't feel shy in the asking because you will be returning the favor. This exchange of information, contacts or ideas occurs in professional organizations, social clubs, conferences, bars, and so on. Your involvement in the community, your social relationships, and your general acquaintances are all contact possibilities.

Information Interviews: The interview for information is an excellent method for acquiring detailed and specific facts and knowledge. You interview people who are in jobs, fields or companies you would like to explore. You are *not* interviewing for a job but are seeking information about the field or company. Before beginning the process, you should narrow your career alternatives by exhausting the information resources at your library or career center. Then you are ready to interview.

The first step is to find the right person to interview. Initially it may seem like an impossible task. Be creative. Tell everyone you know what fields or jobs you would like to explore. Spread the word. Someone you know may have a friend who is in the field you want to explore. If you are unable to find an interviewee with this method, try the phonebook, professional organizations, or chamber of commerce listings.

Handle the interview process in a professional manner. Dress as if you were going to interview for a job. Schedule an appointment that is mutually convenient—you do not want to impose. Plan to meet at the interviewee's place of employment in order to experience, firsthand, the work environment. I once interviewed an art teacher at an elementary school. We met in her spacious classroom. It was brightly decorated, had rows of easels and was filled with art supplies. I felt at home. But when the bell rang, thirty screaming children ran into the classroom. It was chaos. I immediately knew this was not the environment for me. If it's not possible for you to visit your interviewee's place of employment, offer to take her to lunch, and pick her up at work so you can briefly witness the environment.

Prepare well for the interview. You should not only know about the field but also something about the individual you are interviewing. Come equipped with questions. Bring a notebook, or ask in advance if you may record the interview. The more prepared you are, the better results you will have and the better impression you will leave. If you plan to pursue that field or enter employment with that organization, tell your interviewee that you are interested in the type of work she does or in the company. Ask for other contacts or resources. Ask to whom you might talk about job possibilities in the field or with that firm. People who are content and confident in their

147

jobs will be happy to help you. Show your interest by asking permission to leave your resume in case a job opens.

Use tact when interviewing someone about her job. Do not make her feel that she is being used, and do not threaten her position with the company. The reason you are there is to find out whether or not you would like that kind of job.

Most important of all is to be yourself. In your career-development process, you want to come out of the closet and show your true self. Use good etiquette and write your interviewee a note thanking her for her time. If you were particularly enthusiastic about the results of the interview, be sure to let her know.

Table 5: Some Resources for Career Research

Printed

California Occupational Guides

Career Research Monographs

Chronicle Occupational Briefs

COPSystem Career Cluster Booklets

Dictionary of Occupational Titles (DOT)

Encyclopedia of Careers

Guide for Occupational Exploration (GOE)

Occupational Outlook Handbook (OOH)

Vocational Biographies

Worker Trait Group Guide

Audio-Visual

Eureka
Vital Information for Education and Work (VIEW)

Computer Software

Career Planning System Eureka

System Interactive Guidance Information (SIGI)

Exercises

A. Career Exploration

Investigate several occupations by following these steps for each field of interest:

1. Summarize the job duties and responsibilities, work environment, salary/benefits, and working hours.

2. Summarize the skills and education required, and the methods of entry into this field.

3. Discuss the skills you have that are necessary for this field.

4. Describe the skills you need to acquire to enter this field. How will you acquire these skills?

5. Describe how this occupation specifically does or does not match your values, interests, skills, and personality.

B. Information Interview

Make an appointment to interview someone who works in a job that you would like to explore in more detail. Use questions from the list below.

- How did you get into this field?

- What training or academic preparation did you have?

- What do you like most/least about your job?

- What are your responsibilities?

- Are these duties the same for everyone with this job title?

- Describe your typical day.

- What personal qualities do you feel are important in your work?

- What are the prospects for someone like me to enter your field today?

- What advice would you give me to go about applying for and finding a job in this field?

- What kind of salary would I expect in this field?

- Can you suggest someone else to contact to find out more about this field?

- Are there publications I should know of, or professional organizations I should join?

- What are the values and philosophy of this firm, or of the people in this field?

- What type of person would fit best in this type of work?

- Why did you choose this occupation?

Profile: Paula Dombrowski

A. Career Exploration

I researched the field of fashion design.

1. Fashion designers begin with an idea for which they design a flat pattern. They research trends by attending shows or visiting shops. They keep abreast on foreign fashions, new textiles, colors, trimmings and accessories. The workpace is fast and pressured. Beginners start in the workroom, where they cut, drape, sew, make patterns or construct garments. Others may find jobs as sketchers, copyists or trainees in design rooms. Beginners should accept any job they can in the industry.

   In addition to the duties above, custom designers, who own their own shops, hire and supervise staff, promote and take care of business details. They create exclusive designs for a select clientele or work for specialty shops.

   The hours vary from a nine-to-five setting to long evening hours in preparing for shows. During slower times, designers travel. Assistant designers begin at a salary as low as $350 per week, whereas well-known designers in top firms can earn $100,000 per year or more.

   Most fashion designers work for apparel manufacturing firms. Garment districts are located primarily in New York and Los Angeles. The employment outlook has declined since the seventies because foreign products have taken over.

Paula (continued)

2. Skills and education required: Knowledge of textiles, sewing and clothing construction, pattern-making techniques and fashion trends; good sense of color and form; ability to draw; creativity; an ability to synthesize and express ideas. These skills can be acquired through a college program in fashion design or through on-the-job training or a combination of the above.

3. I have all these skills but need more experience.

4. I need to learn more about textile chemistry and applications, clothing construction and marketing techniques. I could enter a fashion design program at a college for a degree. I could take the specific courses in the skills I need, which would include many business skills I believe are necessary to be successful.

5. This occupation fits my personality because it would allow me to be creative, use and express my ideas, work with people and fulfill my interest in fashion. I already have the creative and some of the technical skills required. It fulfills my work values of creativity, independence (if I had my own shop, not if I had to work under someone, which is often the case), and aesthetics. I know it is a competitive field. Hours do not fit a family life. Most fashion centers are in large metropolitan areas. I would not want to commute to the city.

Profile: Maureen Casey

B. Information Interview

I interviewed Mary Nelis, an outdoor guide.

MC: How did you get into this field?

MN: I have been involved in outdoor activities such as backpacking, canoeing, hiking, kayaking, and biking since I was a kid. I enjoy the outdoors and physical challenges. I went to college to become a forest ranger but became disillusioned because of the law enforcement aspect. After I quit, I did odd jobs and volunteered for the YWCA. I landed a position as an activities coordinator for a community center. Through that position, I met a man who took people on nature hikes and natural history outings. I attended all of his outings and eventually became his aid. After a year I decided to start my own business. Over the next year, I attended several small business workshops, consulted the Small Business Administration and researched my market. I decided to focus my business on mountain activities, such as cross-country skiing and snowshoeing trips in the winter, and river rafting and backpacking during the summer.

MC: How did you get started? How much money did it take?

MN: I started with $6,000. The first year, I kept my job and offered three- and four-day trips and a few week-long trips. I took vacation time for these trips. I invested in brochures, mailing lists and equipment. My first groups were mainly solicited by friends who work at outdoor equipment stores. Through word of mouth, the business expanded. It took two years before I could earn enough to quit my regular job.

154

Maureen (continued)

MC: What do and don't you like about the work?

MN: After three years, I found that I spent more time doing business and marketing than trips. I hired an assistant and took on a college student to help with marketing. That was my best move, because it freed me from the stress I was feeling. My student designed a plan to solicit corporations and offer meeting-vacations in the serenity of the mountains. I bought a suit and some nylons and approached them with the idea. The fees they paid allowed me to upgrade equipment.

MC: Do you have any suggestions for starting a related business?

MN: Research your market. Take small business classes at a local college. Get advice from accountants and lawyers. Tell everyone you know about your business before you even start (get the word out). Have enough start-up money. Be sure you are willing to work eighty hours per week in the beginning.

Profile: Maria Diego

A. Career Exploration

I researched the field of physical therapy.

1. A physical therapist improves mobility, relieves pain and prevents or limits the permanent disability of patients suffering from injuries or disease. She reviews each patient's medical history and determines treatment. A physical therapist uses exercise, weights, heat, electricity or ultrasound to relieve pain or improve conditions of muscles. The therapist must keep records of each patient's progress for insurance, legal, and medical team conferences. Most physical therapists work in hospitals and thus have varied hours, including nights and weekends. They also work in nursing homes, for home healthcare organizations, rehabilitation centers, sports medicine clinics and school districts with disabled children. Related fields are athletic trainer, message therapist or chiropractor. Salaries start from $22,000 to $35,000 depending on where you live and your experience. The outlook is excellent, but master's degree programs have limited enrollment. You need good grades and previous experience.

2. Currently, most bachelor-level PT programs are changing to master-level programs. To enter these, you need a degree in biology, nursing or related field. Coursework includes anatomy, physiology, chemistry, human growth, and therapeutic procedures. Personal skills include traits such as patience, tact, persuasiveness, resourcefulness and emotional stability. You need dexterity, physical strength and agility. You are also expected to volunteer or work part-time as an aide.

Maria *(continued)*

3. I have the personal characteristics, and aptitude and interest in science, manual dexterity, physical stamina and a background in the medical field.

4. I need more background in human anatomy and physiology and the technical skills of this field, which I could learn through formal education and through exposure to the field.

5. Physical therapy matches my interests in helping people and in the medical field. I must be efficient, personable, nurturing, accommodating, influential and collaborative. This field fits my values because I can help others and have financial security. It's also in my field of interest and allows for association with colleagues in a professional manner. I will use skills I most prefer, such as treating, acting as liaison, motivating, dealing with feelings and teaching. The main disadvantage is the number of years of schooling and the types of hours I may need to work.

Profile: Sara Harris

---

1. Information Interview

I interviewed Crystal Poe, a game developer.

> SH: How did you get started?

> CP: I taught English for many years and eventually became dissatisfied. I explored fields in which I could have more independence and use my writing skills. I had completed six months of a technical writing training program when I was in a major auto accident. Unable to move about, I had a lot of free time to think. This is when the idea for my first game came to me. With the help of a friend, who designed the graphics for the game, I distributed it among friends and family. Everyone urged me to sell it to a game company. So I did.

> Meanwhile, I recovered and needed to go back to work. I finished the technical writing program, which, by the way, did help me with writing instructions to the game. More ideas came to me, which I worked on during free time. My graphic artist friend and I collaborated again and produced another game. We did this while working our regular jobs. We decided to produce and market this game ourselves.

> SH: How did you sell your game?

> CP: I looked in education stores for games with a similar theme as mine, then checked which companies sold them. I presented my ideas to these companies, and I explained how I had used the game. I also had testimonials from people who liked and used my game.

Sara (continued)

SH: How did you market the games you produced?

CP: Attended educational conferences and conventions. Put ads in trade journals and catalogs.

SH: How did you know that you would be successful?

CP: I didn't know. It sounds simplistic as I tell you from hindsight. The truth is, I worked on the project because it was fun. I had positive collaborative help. I believed in what I was doing. As games were selling and new ideas flowed in, I had less time for my regular job and made the decision to quit.

SH: What are some of the practical business aspects of your work?

CP: Knowing how to evaluate the market and adapt my ideas. Knowing where to find help and when to hire outside to do work such as packaging, distributing or bookkeeping and processing orders. Knowing when to risk. I'm not very practical; I base a lot of my decisions on gut feelings.

SH: What kind of person does it take to develop a new product?

CP: Someone who is creative, self-motivated, organized, persistent, courageous, confident, trusting, willing to take risks.

SH: Can you give me any advice or suggestions? Are there other people I should meet?

CP: You are talking to a person who did not go into this in a logical and calculated manner. You may want to talk to someone who will give you the side I still don't pay much attention to. I have some contacts for you.

CHAPTER IX

Researching Education Opportunities

Lifelong Learning

TO SOME, EDUCATION SEEMS LIKE AN obstacle course to be completed before reaching the goal. The most common obstacles are money, time and previous negative experiences with education.

Without expounding on the benefits of education of and by itself, schooling frequently makes a difference and provides the credentials for many jobs. You may feel more encouraged if you view education as an investment in yourself. You may not always secure the same kind of speedy financial returns as in other investments, but you will gain many personal returns, like self-confidence, a sense of accomplishment, the opportunity to work in the field you want, recognition, purposeful employment, and so on.

You may ask, "How do I go about getting a lengthy education, still have time for home and family, and earn enough to pay the bills?"

It is challenging, but not impossible. In the Resources section of this book, study the available materials on scholarships and financial aid. Many scholarships go unused because people are not aware they exist or think they will not be eligible. Non-traditional educational programs offer, among other things, course schedules that fit into the agenda of working adults.

Traditional Education

SCHOOLS ARE GENERALLY ARRANGED into these five categories, determined by the degrees they offer:

- doctorate granting

- comprehensive universities and colleges

- liberal arts colleges

- two-year colleges

- institutions for non-traditional study

Universities and colleges are also separated into public institutions (funding by public means) or private institutions (privately funded). Colleges grant bachelor (four-year) degrees in liberal arts and sciences. Universities have research facilities and, in addition to providing bachelor programs, offer professional degrees as in law or medicine, and graduate studies toward master's and doctorate degrees. Community, junior, vocational or two-year colleges provide training in specialized (vocational) fields that take six months to three years to complete. They offer associate degrees in vocational areas, in liberal arts and in sciences. You can also prepare to transfer to a bachelor-granting (four-year) college by spending your first two years at a junior college. Community colleges also offer remedial training in math, English and reading in order to prepare you for college-level courses.

Vocational training programs focus primarily on the actual skills you need for an occupation. For instance, a construction technology program will offer courses that teach skills and techniques for

162

entering a job in that field. A nursing program will offer the training and knowledge to become a nurse. You may focus on developing skills for a particular occupation by completing a Certificate of Proficiency, which takes about one year, or by completing specialized courses along with general education courses and receiving an associate's degree, which takes about two years of full-time study.

Both two-year and four-year colleges offer technical degrees and liberal arts degrees in areas such as humanities, social sciences, arts and business. The purpose of a liberal arts education is to train you in interpersonal, self-management and critical-thinking skills. Interpersonal skills include leadership, problem-solving and communication. Time-management, organization and decision-making are some self-management skills. Critical thinking includes the ability to analyze information, be objective, detect biases and understand other points of view. With these basic skills, you will be prepared for a wide variety of management or administrative positions and have the background to enter many fields of employment. Liberal arts students are also trained in other functional skills for a variety of occupations (see chapter five), in which the specific knowledge or technical skills can be learned on the job.

All degree-granting colleges and universities require general education for associate- and bachelor-level degrees. General education normally includes courses in English, math, humanities, natural sciences and social sciences. Each institution has its own particular requirements that may or may not match those of other institutions. Therefore, when you are changing or transferring colleges, you need to know the courses that the other college requires. Academic advisors can assist you with the requirements for degrees and with transfer information.

Traditional colleges use two different calendars. The semester calendar consists of two semesters per year, which range from fifteen to eighteen weeks each. The fall semester begins in August or September and ends in mid-December or mid-January; the spring semester begins in January and ends in May or June. The quarter calendar lasts ten to twelve weeks each, with three (not four) quarters per academic year. First quarter begins in September or October and ends in mid-December; second quarter begins in January; third quarter begins in March or April and ends in June. Both systems offer summer courses, which normally are compressed and more intensive.

For more information on colleges and majors, consult the Resources section at the end of this book.

Alternative Education

ALTERNATIVES TO TRADITIONAL COLLEGE education exist and are well-suited for working adults. As more adults need education, college systems will flex to comply with their needs. The median age for community college students in California is thirty-three and rising. Many colleges now offer evening, Saturday and accelerated courses. Institutions will continue to adapt as more adults enter their programs.

Research the opportunities for alternative education programs such as the following:

- correspondence or independent study programs

- credit by exam

- credit for life experience

- alternative degree programs

The alternative education approach requires self-motivation and self-discipline. Since these programs have less structure and no defined system to follow, you must create your own. Non-traditional programs are designed to fit your needs and incorporate your experience. They could save you time and money.

Correspondence or Independent Study: These courses are completed at home. You read and study the material on your own. When you have questions, you write them out to the instructor or call for a mini-conference. Several large college institutions offer correspondence courses, which can apply toward associate or bachelor degrees. Ask the school from which you intend to receive your degree whether they accept correspondence courses. College administration limits the number of units of correspondence work they will accept. Correspondence courses can supplement your regular classes during periods when you have free time, such as the summer or during long holiday breaks. You must, however, be inspired to complete this work on your own. See the Resources section for where to write for the Directory of Accredited Home Study Schools.

Credit by Exam: You can receive college credit by examination with the College Level Examination Program (CLEP) through the College Entrance Board. The Board sends released scores to colleges and universities, who grant you the credit. The General Exam covers English composition, mathematics, humanities, natural sciences and social sciences/history. The Subject Exams cover forty-seven subjects in business, dental auxiliary education, humanities, education, mathematics, medical technology, nursing, natural sciences and social sciences. See the Resources section for where to write for more information about CLEP.

Credit for Life Experience: Some colleges offer credit for your life experiences. You may receive credit for experiences in several areas such as volunteer work, homemaking, travel, non- credit courses, work, hobbies and other avocations, or personal extensive studies through reading or fieldwork. To receive credit, identify what you have learned and illustrate how it corresponds to particular courses described in the college's catalog and degree programs. Document your proposal by submitting transcripts, letters from employers and supervisors, examples of work and essays demonstrating that you understand the theoretical concepts. You must interpret your knowledge into existing college course outlines. Some colleges have counselors to help you document this information. You may also receive credit by taking an equivalency exam to demonstrate your knowledge.

External Degree Programs: These programs are earned primarily off-campus through correspondence, television courses, credit by exam, and credit for life experience. Normally, external programs combine many of these methods with some traditional on-campus course work. For more information, consult the Resources section of this book.

Certificate Programs: Students wanting to focus on a specialized field may often do so by completing a certificate program. These programs are direct routes into fields that do not require degrees, or they provide the skills for entry-level positions in a field. In the latter case, you can apply courses toward a degree at a later date.

Learning Contract: An innovative approach in alternative education is called the learning contract. It is a formal arrangement between you and the institution, which describes your educational goals and the methods you will take to achieve this goal. The contract includes any of the above methods of learning and obtaining credit.

How to Pay for Your Education

NOW THAT YOU KNOW SOMETHING ABOUT colleges and alternative education, you may still be wondering how you can afford school. There are four general possibilities for funding your education:

- Financial Aid

- Scholarships

- Grants

- Loans

Financial aid goes to those who cannot afford the cost of education on their own. Scholarships are gifts of money or tuition waivers, usually based on academic excellence but also based on particular interests and background. Scholarships are offered through various sources, such as religious, social or fraternal groups, and by individuals, businesses and professional organizations. Scholarships are also offered through the college institution. Grants are gifts of money or tuition waivers that are usually based on financial need. Loans are normally advanced directly by outside lenders and are paid after graduation at an interest rate that is lower than the current prime rate. Some government agencies provide forgivable loans to their employees or potential employees, which are worked off through employment with that particular government agency.

Investigate all forms of financial aid. Computer services are available at minimal fees to search out scholarships to match your specific needs, background and interests. If you are willing to spend some time in the library, you can locate these sources of moneys on your own.

Federal Aid: A wide range of federal assistance is available. Check with the financial aid department of your school. Or call the Federal Student Aid Information center at 1-800-333-INFO for the free booklet, *The Student Guide: Five Federal Financial Aid Programs.* The following are different types of federal aid:

- Pell Grants are awarded to undergraduates (students who do not have bachelor degrees) and need not be repaid. Awards are based on need. You must be at least a half-time student (carry six or more units).

- Supplemental Educational Opportunity Grants (SEOG) are awarded to undergraduates only and do not have to be repaid. It is based on student's need.

- College Work-Study provides jobs for students on- and off-campus and is based on student's need.

- Perkins Loan offers low-interest loans based on student's need. Loans need not be repaid until after the student graduates.

- Stafford Loan is another low-interest loan that is paid back after the student leaves college.

- PLUS and SLS Loans are other loan programs with higher interest rates; borrowers do not have to show need.

Follow these important preliminary steps when applying for any type of financial aid:

1. Analyze your financial resources, current support, savings and paid work that you can continue while in school.

2. Assess expenses of your preferred colleges. Be sure to include tuition, books, school supplies and transportation.

3. Check with the financial aid department of each college institution you are considering.

4. Describe yourself objectively in preparation for applying for scholarships and grants. Consider things like race; ethnic background; religion; geographic area; age; marital status; career specialization; special talents (art, music, athletics); disability; union membership; veteran or veteran dependent; employee of a company that sponsors fraternity, sorority, or other social club/group; scholastic achievements; and financial status.

5. Gather information and records on your financial status, academic performance and work experience. To apply for financial aid you will need financial records such as your income tax statement. To apply for scholarships you will need documentation of scholastic achievements in the form of high school and/or college transcripts, letters of recommendation and a resume.

Hints:

- Do not ignore groups that give small amounts.

- Do not get discouraged. It is a long, arduous process.

- Do not think that you aren't good enough or smart enough.

- Apply for anything and everything for which you qualify.

Exercise

Exploring Education

1. Visit your local library, college career center or college library. Ask the reference person for a book on colleges and/or college majors. Find a few colleges that you would like to explore and obtain their catalogs. If the catalog is not available at the library, call or write the college's recruitment office and ask for a catalog or information on their degree programs. Most catalogs cost between $2 and $5, but other information is usually free. Scan the index of the catalog to find your field of interest or to see what majors they offer and the types of courses required for the various majors. Read the course descriptions of the required classes in the major(s) you are interested in. You may be required to take additional courses from departments other than that of your major. Read those descriptions as well. Jot down your impressions of that major. Answer these questions:

   - Which courses seem interesting/ uninteresting?

   - Which courses appear difficult/easy?

   - What is the connection between the courses in my field of interest and the other required courses? (If you don't see a connection, make a note to find out why the courses are required.)

2. Make an appointment with an academic advisor who specializes in your major of interest. Ask the advisor:

- What are the specific requirements for obtaining a degree in my interest area (major)?

- What other requirements do I need to fulfill to obtain a degree?

- What steps do I need to take to enter that college or university?

- How do I get information on financial aid, programs/courses, scholarships, career information, or any other information or services they may offer a person with my needs?

- What career opportunities are there for people in my interest area (major)?

Profile: Paula Dombrowski

Exploring Education

I explored a college that offers degrees for life experiences. Since I am so well-read, I can receive units in English and history by either writing a thesis or taking some examinations. I can also receive credit for my business and design experience. I will need about thirty units (which can be completed in one year attending school full-time) for an Associate of Arts degree in design or merchandising. I must take some math and science and more art and design courses. Some of these can be done by correspondence, others through my local community college; a few specialized courses I must take at this college. Many of their courses are offered on weekends or in week-long intensives.

Profile: Maria Diego

Exploring Education

I made an appointment with a counselor at the local community college to find out what I would need to do to become a nurse and a physical therapist. I discovered that I had several alternatives. I could attend a Licensed Vocational Nursing program, which would take three years, or a Registered Nursing program, which would take four years (including prerequisites to the program). I could also prepare to transfer to a four-year college and receive a bachelor's degree in nursing. Basically, the more education you have, the more you get paid. They also offer a Primary Care Associate program which prepares one to be a Physician's Assistant. To enter this program, I would need previous training in nursing or some other medical field such as paramedic or medical assisting. Although I like the idea of getting a bachelor's degree, this program seems more practical and direct because I would take very few general education courses and more in my field.

The beginning-level courses for nursing and physical therapy are similar, primarily physical and biological science classes, and I would not specialize until my last two years in the bachelor's program. Most physical therapy programs are at the master's degree level. Either a nursing degree or a degree in biology would best prepare me for the physical therapy degree.

I have a good chance of receiving a scholarship and financial aid because I fall into a disadvantaged category and because there is money available to encourage women entering the medical field. I still have a lot to consider and will talk to more people in the medical field.

CHAPTER X

Making a Choice by Fulfilling Your Dreams

It is best to not rush, push yourself or panic when making big decisions. Whenever you can, give yourself the opportunity to try the methods in the exercises below. You will find that a thorough and relaxed decision-making process normally leads to better results. On the other hand, you may feel tempted to stay in the researching options and contemplation stages in order to put off making a move. If this is the case, do not get down on yourself for being unable to decide, but try to uncover what is holding you back. For most people, it is fear. There are many kinds of fear, and how to deal with these is not in the scope of this book. Seek out supportive friends or professionals, or read literature relating to fear. In most circumstances, if you allow yourself space and time, you can effectively use the decision-making methods described in this chapter.

Using the Left and Right Sides of Your Brain

AN EFFECTIVE METHOD FOR DECISION-making is to combine the energies of both the left and right side of your brain. The left-brain is the rational, logical, linear and analytical part of you. The right-brain is the intuitive, creative, spacial and imaginative part of you. Your left-brain is needed for analyzing the alternatives, realizing consequences and calculating risks. It is also essential for investigating all your options and questioning the alternatives. The right-brain assists in brainstorming alternatives that may, at first, not be apparent. It will also reveal what you truly desire in spite of the risks. And finally, after all your calculating, thinking, and analyzing, it can provide that "hunch" and enlighten you about a solution. In order to balance and utilize both parts of your brain, use the decision-making model outlined below. Before you use any of your left-brain strengths such as analyzing and discerning, try the guided visualization exercise, Decision by Intuition, which will help unleash your right-brain intuitive process.

Exercises

A. Decision by Intuition[1]

First, think of a decision you want to make. Choose two to five options for that decision. Number each option.

Now use the relaxation exercise in the appendix.

Imagine yourself walking down a country road. You feel confident and expectant as you enjoy your walk. Hear the leaves crackling under your feet. As the sun shines through the trees, it warms your face and body. At the end of the road is a cottage. You find yourself drawn to it. You walk inside to find a long hallway with several doors. You know that something important is behind each of these doors; each door represents one of the options for your decision.

Open the first door and walk into the room. You experience the first option for your decision, either symbolically or in actuality. What do you experience? How does it feel to be in that room? What are your senses telling you? Spend as much time as you need in the room to get a good sense of how that option feels. Leave the room, close the door, and know that you may return if you wish.

Now open the next door, which represents your second option, which you experience either symbolically or in actuality. How does it feel to be in that room? What do you find there? What are your senses telling you? Spend as much time as necessary to experience that option. When you are ready, leave the second room, close the door behind you, and know that you have the option to return if you choose.

Follow the same process until you have entered the room for each option. When you are ready, write what you have experienced.

---

[1] Adapted from Rosanoff, *Intuition Workout*, 29-30.

B. Right- and Left-Brain Decision-Making

Left

1. *Clarify Decision.* Write down all considerations of your decision, so you are clear about what you are deciding. Writing them out will untangle the many aspects to consider and clear up your opposing feelings. Do not phrase your possible decisions as an either/or option. You want to create several alternatives.

Right

2. *Uncover Feelings.* Identify the feelings surrounding your decision. Sit quietly and use the relaxation technique in the appendix. Concentrate on your body. Where do you feel the conflict regarding the possible decisions? What is your body telling you?

3. *Brainstorm Options.* Either on your own or with others, brainstorm numerous options for your decision. Discover as many options as possible. Never feel rushed or frustrated when creating options. Don't block your creativity. Turn off your censor and be sure not to "yes but" any options that you or others invent.

4. *Research.* For each option you wish to consider, investigate the steps you would need to take to make that option workable. Gather the information you need to determine how well that alternative will work for you. After thorough research of each option, you may find that some are more feasible than others.

5. *Use Intuition.* Use the relaxation technique in the appendix. Shut down the part of you that wants to analyze and figure things out. Call on your intuition by drawing pictures, using symbols or metaphors, exercise or movement, or other creative or somatic processes to uncover answers.

Left

6. Evaluate.

Negative Consequences — Evaluate the consequences for yourself and those around you. Look behind the negativity for personal fear and doubt.

Shoulds — What are your "shoulds" and "ought tos"? Who is telling you that you should or should not?

Risks — How much are you risking and how amenable are you to taking that risk?

Right

7. Evaluate:

Desire — Ask yourself how strongly you desire that choice in spite of risks.

Intention — What is motivating you to go with this option? Imagine the result of your intention.

Feeling — Meditate, use creative or somatic processes to identify and work through negative feelings around options.

8. Relax. Take a break from thinking about the decision. The right-brain, in the unconscious, will continue to work for you. By deliberately not concerning yourself with the decision on a conscious level, your mind will be clear to hear what your intuition wants you to know about the decision. The decision fantasy exercise may help you tap into your intuition. Make sure you take that break! The recess will clear and relax your mind before you review the options. If the perfect solution doesn't come, trust that it will eventually. Look for insight in small places. *Do not* go back to analyzing the situation and forcing a decision.

Left

9. *Decide.* Are you ready? If not, take more time in the previous step. Or review all the steps and see where you need more work. Then review your options anew and decide. In choosing, you must also prepare a plan of action. Write down what steps you need to take to actualize your decision. Include in your choice a time structure to try out your decision. This does not imply that you are not serious about your decision. When you decide, you are positive. But you need to include the possibility of the unknown. You cannot foresee all that may happen. You need to leave an opening for life when it happens as you are living out your decision. You may choose to adapt or modify whatever seems necessary.

Profile: Paula Dombrowski

A. Decision by Intuition

Room One: Full-time job. It was dark and dreary.

Room Two: Part-time job and do my own thing part-time. The room was a mess. I kept falling over things.

Room Three: Start business. Room turned into a large warehouse full of creative supplies. It was exciting, so many things to do. I was overwhelmed.

B. Right- and Left-Brain Decision-Making

1. *Clarify Decision*: The decision is between getting a more practical job and pursuing creative work as a career.

2. *Uncover Feelings*: I feel anxious, depressed and resentful. I don't want to be in the position of making this decision. There is a heavy feeling in the pit of my stomach.

3. *Brainstorm Options*: Options include: sales or buyer job in garment industry, fashion designer, open my own shop, represent other artist's work, do part-time job in sales or people-related area, do art during my own time, go to college to discover myself, move to an art community.

4. *Research*: Interviewed a buyer and a retail sales rep. Went to a How to Start Your Own Business workshop. Talked to artists. Saw counselor at a college. I could research more.

5. *Use Intuition*: Three categories of options:
a. Full-time work for someone else;
b. Part-time low-stress and part-time my-own-thing; or
c. Go out on a limb and go for it!

181

Paula (continued)

---

6. *Evaluate:*

Negative Consequences —

a. Will not like working for someone else, rigid schedule, high stress, low creativity.

b. May end up floundering the few hours per day left to do my own thing. May dislike part-time work too much. May not do well at either. May not earn enough at either.

c. May not succeed.

 Shoulds —

a. Practical, money-making.

b. Less risky.

c. None.

Risk —

a. Too competitive, won't get hired, too stressful.

b. Won't succeed at either.

c. Won't succeed.

7. *Evaluate:*

Desire —

a. To make income. To be out in the world.

b. To not give up on dream, yet be practical.

c. To not give up on dream.

Intention —

a. Do what seems most feasible.

b. Create balance between what I want and what seems practical.

c. Do what I love.

Feeling —

I used a symbol of the lion, which gives me courage.

9. *Decide:* Don't need to decide as yet. Sending out feelers. Will teach a community workshop on Enhancing Your Self-Image and see what kind of response I get. Will take a class in fabric design. Where will this lead?

Profile: Maureen Casey

A. Decision by Intuition

Option One: I move in with Robert. It was Robert's living room. We were arguing over something. I was so angry, I left the room.

Option Two: Robert moves in with me. The room is full of furniture. It's noisy, but cozy. A fire is going in the fireplace.

Option Three: Unknown. The room is light. Music is coming through an open window. I go to it and look outside. I see mountains, pine trees and a lake.

B. Right- and Left-Brain Decision-Making

The issue here is: 1) whether to change jobs and move in with Robert; 2) ask him to move and commute, or change jobs; or 3) both move somewhere in the middle and keep our jobs. This is a difficult decision because I have been independent for so many years and because I want to be near the kids. I feel confident that we will work something out. I admit that I'm nervous taking this step, after so many years being alone. Meanwhile, I introduced an outdoor-trip-for-executives idea at work. Thus, I'm less interested in leaving my job. I would rather stay put, since there are too many consequences for moving (kids, job, and giving up independence).

The risk in staying here and asking Robert to move or commute is that he will resent me or won't be able to find a comparable job here. Then, I may not like living away from the kids, in a new area, and changing jobs all at once. My intention and desire is to create balance between my needs and his needs. This would give us both a more free and open relationship, since neither would be compromising (too much) for the other. I envision harmony and open communication.

Maureen (continued)

I have two opposing shoulds: to move because I am being too selfish, and not to move because women always give up for men. I want to be fair, but I don't want to compromise myself. When thinking about the options and then concentrating on my body, I found my limbs becoming tight. To me, this meant that I'm not ready to move. So I will relax and take my time to decide. Meanwhile, Robert and I can take turns commuting. I may be able to work four-day weeks.

Profile: Maria Diego

A. Decision by Intuition

Room One: Work Full-Time/School Part-Time. It's filled with stacks of books, dishes, laundry. I run from one stack to the next. I'm so worried about the next stack, I leave the one I'm working on undone. Pretty soon I'm exhausted.

Room Two: School Full-Time/Work Part-Time. This room is old and barren.

Room Three: Alternative School Full-Time/Work Part-Time: I am in another hallway. It's dark. I continue to walk, feeling the walls to guide me, and in hope of finding a light switch. I turn many corners. I become frightened. Just as I am ready to turn back to what is familiar, I find a light switch.

B. Right- and Left-Brain Decision-Making

I want to go to school to become a nurse or a physician's assistant. I believe I have a good chance of doing well and getting a job because I am good with people, I enjoy sciences and I speak Spanish (an asset in the health field). I, however, will need three to four years of education. I must decide whether I should go to school full-time or part-time, and whether I should work full-time or part-time, etc. I still feel the pull of my family, who prefer I find a husband rather than fulfill my ambitions.

In my research, I found a private school that offers a three-year program (go to school all year long) for a B.S. in nursing. If I go to work part-time, I will be eligible for financial aid. I also have applied for five scholarships. The risks and consequences for going to work part-time and school full-time are that I won't have enough money. My shoulds are driving me crazy because most of them are saying that I have a comfortable and secure job—why do I want to disrupt my family's life?

Maria (continued)

My desire and intention is to get on with my education and get closer to my goal. On the other hand, the risk/consequence of working full-time and schooling part-time is that it will take too long and I will burn out and give up. The desire/motivation is to have a career that I would enjoy, and in which I could help others and achieve something.

I took a break. It worked! I had a dream: the children and I were on a trip. The car broke down. We were in the desert. I had brought enough food for a day. I made a shelter using Elena's wide skirt. We all pitched in, didn't worry, and had fun. Just as the sun began to set, an old man appeared who towed our car, which turned into a motor home. I will go to school, ask my employers to let me work part-time, apply for loans and scholarships. If worse comes to worse, I will not be able to go full-time, and take only one or two classes. The children can pitch in. I will take it semester by semester.

Profile: Sara Harris

A. Decision by Intuition

Option One: Complete school. The door leads to the outside. I must climb down a steep cliff. When I reach the bottom, there is nothing left but to climb up another one. I persist, reach the top and can see very far.

Option Two: Work part-time in current job. I'm outside again. It's a lovely English garden. I explore and enjoy its beauty. I come to the end of the garden to a wall covered with ivy. As I follow the wall, I realize that it surrounds the garden.

Option Three: Quit school and job to try unknown. I'm back on the cliff. This time, I notice a ledge I can take across to the other side. It opens up to a large field with daffodils.

B. Right- and Left-Brain Decision-Making

I need to consider whether or not to complete my PhD, and if I do, what will I do with it? I need to decide whether to continue current job, find full-time job, part-time job, join the Peace Corps, move to North Dakota (low rent) and write a book, or what else?

My shoulds say, "Finish the degree; it's your ticket." My desire is to do more creative, less analytical work. The risk in quitting school is that I will regret it later and they won't let me come back if I choose to. My intention to go back would be to complete what I've begun, do what's right. But I need a break today.

I researched alternative PhD programs. This could be a future option if I decide to quit now. I wouldn't want to switch schools now. I also looked into part-time college teaching. Pay is poor, but they offer flexibility and independence. Also looked at jobsharing. I know a few people interested in sharing counseling positions. I'm going to go with my desire rather than my shoulds. Even as I write this, I tremble, but inside it feels right. What I do next will depend on jobsharing opportunities, if they extend my current contract, and on the teaching possibilities. I am definitely making a path to try my ideas in creating educational materials.

EPILOGUE

"Just Do It"

Developing a career, following a life mission, finding the perfect balance and being true to yourself is a lifelong and continuing process. When students or clients ask me, "How do I know what is right for me?" or "How can I do what I want when there are so many things against it?" my answer, like the Nike advertisement, is, "Just do it."

In my own personal experience of developing career and other life goals, there have been times when I knew my heart's desire and trusted I would achieve it. There also have been times when I yearned for the time, the money or the opportunity to go in a direction, but could not budge due to fears and shoulds. I've learned that most barriers exist only because I allow them to. When something is unclear or I'm prevented (or preventing myself) from taking on a new direction or challenge, I deliberately find a bit of space in my schedule to "just do it." By making the effort, I begin to realize the value of this new desire or direction, that this is really what I want, that it's actually good for me, and that it really isn't imposing on other parts of my life. Or I find that it wasn't what I wanted, and consequently I discover something else which may be closely related to my initial desire.

All your ideas, desires, and opportunities are there for a reason. You can follow up, check them out, experiment and see what happens. All of these will eventually get you to where you are going. There is no wrong turn. One option will give you the kind of experience that leads to another, and so on. As the saying goes, "All roads lead to Rome."

What's important in trying an idea or career direction is that you pay close attention to your *intention* and your *feelings*. Consider shoulds, wants, fears, risks, and consequences. Ask yourself:

- Why am I considering this direction?
- Whom will this please?
- How do I feel about this option?
- What is the intention underlying this choice?

When you are in tune with yourself, you eventually are more able to fine-tune your goals and visions. So treat your past experiences as lessons in life. See your present as an opportunity to be who you are and do what you love. The future will unfold from there.

If there is something your heart desires, take ten minutes to an hour per day doing what you want. In this way, you will show your inner self what direction you intend to go. You are also affirming to yourself that you *may* have what you want. In process, you will find yourself feeling fulfilled, motivated, confident and driven not only toward your new goal but in other areas of your life.

Profile: Paula Dombrowski

Paula is looking through sketches she has prepared for a new client, Phil Van Horn. She puts her sketches in order and cleans up the studio/office in preparation for her meeting with the young and unmarried Mr. Van Horn. She is tempted to introduce this successful entrepreneur to her daughter, but knows better. Paula prepares her color chart with separate swatches of fabric for suits and shirts and for leisure wear.

The idea of helping men choose clothing began when her son graduated from college and needed clothing for his interviews. She helped many of his friends choose versatile clothing. She then proposed to do a dress-for-success on a low budget for male students interviewing and seeking their first professional jobs. For a minimal fee, she helped many students shop and began to build a reputation in the community.

Profile: Maureen Casey

"Is that the last of it?" Robert asks as he put a box into the van.

"Yes, thanks." Maureen answers. "Sure glad I got that storage space in Bear Canyon. Saves a lot of time." She closed the van door and turned to kiss her husband good bye. "See you up there Saturday night."

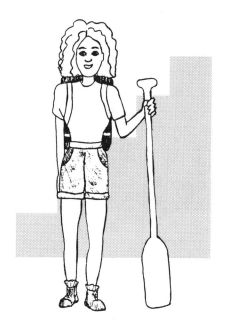

"Can't wait," he returns.

Maureen pulls out of the dirt driveway of their home in Nevada City. Her drive to Bear Canyon is a little shy of two hours. She will meet her group of engineers for a three-day river-rafting trip at the lodge. Robert will join them at the halfway point, downriver.

Robert and Maureen discovered this mountainous area on their way home from a skiing trip. Robert quit his fast-paced job and downshifted to a less prestigious law firm, a forty-five minute commute down the mountain. At first reluctant, Maureen also left her job. She spent a year fixing up their new home and preparing for her Mountain Tours business. Using her own contacts and those from Robert's previous job, she was able to make ends meet the first year. Now she is building a reputation through the local tourist industry in her own town.

Profile: Maria Diego

It is hard for Maria to believe that only five years ago she was interviewing a physician's assistant in trying to decide whether she wanted to go back to school. Today, Maria is interviewing for a job in a mobile clinic. She will assist migrant workers with health problems. In a different city each day of the week, Maria's place of employment will cover over one hundred miles. She is a finalist in the interview process because of her experience working in clinics, her attitude and her bilingual skills.

After on-the-job training in medical assisting, Maria continued to work in her medical office while pursuing a degree in primary care as a physician's assistant. She was able to receive a full scholarship for her three years of training, and she joined a forgivable loan program in which she would promise to work community service hours. In return, her county would pay off her loan. She also joined a mentor program affiliated with the community college and met Francisca Ponce, a public health educator and activist. Maria has found her niche and is able to help her community in ways she had not anticipated. Recently, she has been asked to volunteer as a mentor and speak to the new class of graduating nurses.

Profile: Sara Harris

The L-shaped work area faces a picture window that looks out on the flower garden. On the horizontal side of the L is Sara's computer equipment and a picture of her two-year-old daughter, Charlotte. Up against this desk, stretching into the vertical line of her L is a long and narrow table with several opened books and other piles, placed there in a seemingly haphazard fashion. She's on the phone with her jobsharing partner discussing the problems and events of the  preceding week. Sara works every other week at a home for unwed mothers. It sometimes is difficult to leave her work problems for an entire week. Sara and her partner have agreed to keep phone calls to one or two per week.

In part, as a result of her work with teenage to-be-mothers, Sara has developed short work booklets on self-esteem. Together with the women at the home, she has designed a game which incorporates the techniques she teaches in her self-esteem workshops.

Relaxation Technique for Guided Visualizations

Sit or lie down in a comfortable position. Close your eyes. Allow your body to relax and allow tension to leave your body. Now breathe deeply and slowly. Experience deeper relaxation with each breath. Breathe in slowly and deeply and bring your breath into your toes and feet. Feel the muscles of your toes and feet relaxing as your breath massages away tension. Breathe in deeply and allow your breath to fill your calves. As you breathe out, feel the tension leave your calves. Now breathe in slowly and deeply into your knees and thighs. Feel your muscles relax as you exhale the tension. Your legs and feet are totally relaxed.

Breathe in slowly and let your breath move into your hips and stomach area. Feel yourself relax and the tension leave your body as you breathe. Now let your breath fill up you chest. Feel your chest expand as you inhale and then relax as you exhale. Now breathe relaxation into your back. Feel the breath flow down each vertebra, slowly massaging your muscles into relaxation as the tension leaves your body. You feel very calm and relaxed.

Breathe in slowly and let your breath move into your hands and fingers. Feel the breath massage the muscles. Breathe in slowly and deeply, allowing the breath to move into your forearms and upper arms. As you exhale, feel your muscles relax and the tension leave your arms. Now feel your legs, arms and torso relax and sink into the ground below.

Breathe in slowly and let your breath massage your shoulders and neck. Feel them relax as you exhale away the tension. Breathe in deeply and allow your breath to fill your head. Feel the breath move up your chin, lips, nose, eyes, forehead and around your skull as if tiny fingers were massaging away tension.

Breathe in deeply and let your body totally relax. Find any part of your body that is tense and allow it to relax. Continue to follow your breathing. You are totally relaxed and comfortable with yourself.

RESOURCES

Women's Career Resources

Cardozo, Arlene Rossen. *Sequencing*. New York: Macmillan Publishing Company, 1986.

Gerson, Kathleen. *Hard Choices: How Women Decide about Work, Career, and Motherhood*. Berkeley: University of California Press, 1985.

Gray, Francine Du Plessix. *Soviet Women: Walking the Tightrope*. New York: Doubleday, 1990.

Gutek, Barbara, and Laurie Larwood. *Women's Career Development*. Newbury Park, California: Sage Publications, 1987.

Josefowitz, Natasha. *Paths to Power: A Woman's Guide from First Job to Top Executive*. Reading, Massachusetts: Addison-Wesley, 1980.

Loden, Marilyn. *Feminine Leadership, or How to Succeed in Business without Being One of the Boys*. New York: Times Books, 1985.

Lunneborg, Patricia. *Women Changing Work*. New York: Bergin & Garvey Publishers, 1990.

Martin, Molly. *Hard Hatted Women: Stories of Struggles & Success in the Trades.* Seattle: Seal Press Feminist, 1988.

Nieva, Veronica, and Barbara Gutek. *Women and Work: A Psychological Perspective.* New York: Praeger Publishers, 1981.

Sloan Fader, Shirley. *From Kitchen to Career: How Any Woman Can Skip Low-Level Jobs and Start in the Middle or at the Top.* New York: Stein & Day, 1977.

United States Department of Labor, Women's Bureau. *Facts on Women Workers: Fact Sheet 88-1.* Washington DC: United States Government Printing Office, January 1988.

Ward, Terry. *Smart Women at Work: 12 Steps to Career Breakthroughs.* Chicago: Contemporary Books, 1987.

Weiner, Lynn Y. *From Working Girl to Working Mother: The Female Labor Force in the United States, 1820-1980.* Chapel Hill: University of North Carolina, 1985.

General Career Resources

Berg, Astrid. *Career Metamorphosis.* Capitola, California: Sefa Books, 1990.

———. *Creatavision.* Capitola, California: Sefa Books, 1991.

Bolles, Richard Nelson. *What Color Is Your Parachute? A Practical Manual for Job-Hunters and Career-Changers.* Berkeley, California: Ten Speed Press. Updated annually.

Figler, Howard, PhD. *The Complete Job-Search Handbook.* New York: Henry Holt and Company, 1979.

Jaffe, Dennis, PhD, and Cynthia Scott, PhD, MPH. *Take This Job and Love It: How to Change Your Work Without Changing Your Job.* New York: Simon & Schuster, 1988.

Handy, Charles. *The Age of Unreason.* Cambridge, Massachusetts: Harvard Business School Press, 1990.

Holland, John L. *Making Vocational Choices: A Theory of Vocational Personalities and Work Environments.* Englewood Cliffs, New Jersey: Prentice-Hall, Inc., 1985.

Morgan, Hal, and Kerry Tucker. *Companies That Care: The Most Family Friendly Companies in America—What They Offer and How They Got That Way.* New York: Fireside, 1991.

Naisbitt, John, and Patricia Aburdene. *Megatrends 2000: Ten New Directions for the 1990s.* New York: William Morrow and Company, Inc., 1990.

Schor, Juliet. *The Overworked American: The Unexpected Decline of Leisure.* New York: Harper Collins Publishers, 1991.

Sher, Barbara. *Wishcraft: How to Get What You Really Want.* New York: Ballantine Books, 1979.

Sinetar, Marsha. *Do What You Love, The Money Will Follow: Discovering Your Right Livelihood.* New York: Dell, 1987.

Weitzen, H. Skip. *Infropreneurs: Turning Data into Dollars.* New York: John Wiley & Sons, Inc., 1988.

Women's Psychology/Self-Help Resources

Belenky, Mary Field, Blythe McVicker Clinchy, Nancy Rule Goldberger, and Jill Mattuck Tarule. *Women's Ways of Knowing: The Development of Self, Voice and Mind.* New York: Basci Books, 1986.

Bianchi, Suzanne, and Daphne Spain. *American Women in Transition.* New York: Russell Sage Foundation, 1986.

Cardoza, Anne DeSola, and Mavis B. Sutton. *Winning Tactics for Women over Forty: How to Take Charge of Your Life and Have Fun Doing It.* Bedford: Mills and Sanderson, Publishers, 1988.

de Castillejo, Irene Claremont. *Knowing Woman: A Feminine Psychology.* Boston: Shambhala, 1990.

Estés, Clarissa Pinkola, PhD. *Women Who Run with Wolves: Myths & Stories of the Wild Woman's Archetype.* New York: Ballantine, 1992.

Faludi, Susan. *Backlash: The Undeclared War Against Women.* New York: Doubleday, 1991.

Gilligan, Carol. *In a Different Voice.* Cambridge: Harvard University Press, 1982.

Lenz, Elinor, and Barbara Myerhoff. *The Feminization of America: How Women's Values Are Changing Our Public and Private Lives.* Los Angeles: Jeremy P. Tarcher, 1977.

Miller, Jean Baker, MD. *Toward a New Psychology of Women*. Second ed. Boston: Beacon Press, 1986.

Steinem, Gloria. *Revolution from Within: A Book of Self-Esteem*. Boston: Little, Brown and Company, 1992.

Woolger, Jennifer Barker and Roger. *The Goddess Within: A Guide to Eternal Myths That Shape Women's Lives*. New York: Fawcett Columbine, 1989.

General Psychology/Self-Help Resources

Bolen, Jean Shinoda, MD. *The Tao of Psychology: Sychronicity and the Self*. San Francisco: HarperCollins Publishers, 1979.

Csikszentmihalya, Mihaly. *Flow: The Psychology of Optimal Experience*. New York: Harper and Row, 1990.

Eisler, Riane, and David Loye. *The Partnership Way: New Tools for Living and Learning, Healing Our Families, Our Communities and Our World*. San Francisco: HarperCollins Publishers, 1990.

Hudson, Frederic. *The Adult Years: Mastering the Art of Self-Renewal*. San Francisco: Bass, Inc., 1991.

Jeffers, Susan. *Feel the Fear and Do It Anyway*. New York: Fawcett, 1988.

Levinson, Daniel. *The Seasons of a Man's Life*. New York: Alfred A. Knopf, 1978.

Maslow, Abraham. *Motivation and Personality*. New York: Harper and Row, 1954.

Myers, Isabel Briggs. *Gifts Differing*. Palo Alto, California: Consulting Psychologist Press, 1980.

Murphy, Elizabeth. *The Developing Child: Using Jungian Type to Understand Children*. Palo Alto, California: Consulting Psychologist Press, 1992.

Rosanoff, Nancy. *Intuition Workout*. Boulder Creek, California: Aslan Publishing, 1988.

Zukav, Gary. *Seat of the Soul*. New York: Simon & Schuster, 1989.

Alternative Workstyles Resources

Arden, Lynie. *Work-at-Home Sourcebook: How to Find "At Home" Work That's Right for You.* 4th ed. Boulder, Colorado: Live Oak, 1992.

————. *Worksteader News.* Quarterly newsletter. Write to 2396 Coolidge Way, Rancho Cordova, California 95670.

Brabec, Barbara. *Homemade Money.* Whitehall, Virginia: Betterway Publications, 1989.

Canape, Charlene. *The Part-Time Solution.* New York: HarperCollins, 1991. Write to Center for Home-Based Businesses, Business Assistance Center, Truman College, 1145 West Wilson Avenue, Chicago, Illinois 60640. (312) 989-6112.

Gordon, Gil, and Marica Kelly. *Telecommunting: How to Make It Work for You and Your Company.* Englewood Cliffs, New Jersey: Prentice-Hall, 1986.

Kirsch, M. M. *How to Get Off the Fast Track and Live the Life That Money Can't Buy.* Los Angeles: Lowell House, 1991.

Lee, Patricia. *The Complete Guide to Job Sharing.* New York: Walker and Company, 1983.

Morgan, Peg. *Invest in Yourself: A Woman's Guide to Starting Her Own Business.* Garden City, New York: Doubleday & Company, Inc., 1983.

O'Hara, Bruce. *Put Work in Its Place: How to Redesign Your Job to Fit Your Life.* Victoria, British Columbia: Work Well Publications, 1988.

Olmsted, Barney, and Suzanne Smith. *Creating a Flexible Workplace: How to Select and Manage Alternative Work Options.* New York: Amacon - American Management Association, 1989.

————. *The Job Sharing Handbook.* Berkeley: Ten Speed Press, 1983.

Ortalda, Robert A., Jr., CPA. *How to Live Within Your Means and Still Finance Your Dreams: A Practical Step-by-Step Program for Taking Charge of Your Financial Future.* New York: Simon & Schuster, 1989.

Work Times: New Ways to Work. Quarterly newsletter. Write to 149 Ninth Street, San Francisco, California 94103.

Education Resources

Bear, John, PhD. *Bear's Guide to Earning Non-Traditional College Degrees.* 11th ed. Berkeley, California: Ten Speed Press, 1990.

College Handbook, The. 30th ed. New York: College Entrance Exam Board, 1993.

Directory of Accredited Home Study Schools. Washington, DC: National Home Study Council. Write to 1601 18th Street NW, Washington, DC 20009.

Guide to CLEP Exams. New York: College Board Publications. Write to College Board Publications, Department B10, Box 866, New York, New York 10101-0886.

Innovative Graduate Programs Directory. 6th ed. Saratoga Springs: New York: Empire State College, 1992. Write to Empire State College, SUNY, Saratoga Springs, New York 12866.

Katz, Montana, and Veronica Vieland. *Get Smart: A Woman's Guide to Equity on Campus.* New York: The Feminist Press, 1988.

Lockheed, Marlaine, Ruth Ekstrom, and Abigail Harris. *How to Get College Credit for What You Have Learned As a Homemaker or Volunteer.* Princeton, New Jersey: Educational Testing Service, 1982.

Mendelsohn, Pam. *Happier by Degrees: The Complete Guide for Women Returning to College or Just Starting Out.* Berkeley: Ten Speed Press, 1986.

Peterson's Guide to Four-Year Colleges. Princeton, New Jersey: Peterson's Guide, updated annually.

Wells, John, and Barbara Ready, eds. *Peterson's: The Independent Study Catalog, the NUCEA Guide to Independent Study Through Correspondence Instruction.* Fourth ed. Washington, DC: Peterson's Guide for the National University of Continuing Education Association, 1989.

Financial Aid Resources

Business and Professional Women's Foundation Educational Programs. Washington, DC: Business and Professional Women, updated annually. Send self-addressed, double-stamped envelope to 2012 Massachusetts Avenue NW, Washington, DC 20036.

Cassidy, Daniel J., and Mildred Alves. *The Scholarship Book*. 3rd ed. Englewood Cliffs, New Jersey: Prentice-Hall, 1990.

Chronicle Student Aid Annual. Moravia, New York: Guidance Publications, updated annually. Write to Aurora Street, PO Box 1190, Moravia, New York 13118.

The College Bluebook: Scholarships, Fellowships, Grants and Loans. 5 vols. New York: Macmillan Publishing Company, updated bi-annually. Write to Macmillan Publishing Company, 866 Third Avenue, New York, New York 10022.

Financial Aid: A Partial List of Resources for Women. Fifth ed. Project of the Status of Resources for Women, Washington, DC: Association of American Colleges, 1991. Write to Association of American Colleges, 1818 R Street NW, Washington, DC 20009.

Hawes, Gene. *The College Board Guide to Going to College While Working: Strategies for Success*. New York: Colleg Board Publications, 1985.

Higher Education Opportunities for Minorities and Women: Annotated Selections. Washington, DC: Government Printing Office, 1991. Write to Superintendent of Documents, Government Printing Office, Washington, DC 20401.

Margolin, Judith. *Financing a College Education: The Essential Guide for the '90s*. New York: Plenum Publishing Corporation, 1989. Write to Plenum Publishing Corporation, 233 Spring Street, New York, New York 10013.

Schlachter, Gail Ann. *Directory of Financial Aid for Women*. San Carlos, California: Reference Service Press, updated bi-annually. Write to Reference Service Press, 1100 Industrial Road, Suite 9, San Carlos, California 94070.

Career Development Workshops
by Astrid Berg

The author of *Finding the Work You Love* is available to come to your school, company, or other community group to speak on the following topics:

For Job Seekers

- **Career Transitions**

- **Alternative Workstyles**

- **Career Goals for the Inner You**

For Career Counselors

- **Using Right-Brain Counseling Techniques**

- **Alternative Directions & Workstyles for Counselors**

- **Counselor Retreats**

Plus Much More!

For more information,
call Career and Life Transitions (408) 462-4626.

More Resources by Astrid Berg

Fishing for Values Card Deck

With this series of games and exercises, players learn to clarify their values and identify their goals. Useful in group settings to facilitate team-building, conflict resolution, and global consciousness. Games include "Values Gin," "Community Values," "Utopia," and "Lifestyles." Available Spring 1994.

2 sets of cards, 1 game booklet, pre-publication price*: $15

Guided Visualization Audiocassette

Listening to this tape can exercise your right-brain ability to both realize and attain your life work or life goals. Includes eleven guided visualizations from the author's books, *Finding the Work You Love* and *Creatavision*. May be used by individuals or in group settings. Available Spring 1994.

60-minute cassette tape, pre-publication price*: $11.95

Pre-publication prices honored through March 31, 1994.

- -

To Order...

...fill out this order form and mail to:

QTY	TITLE	PRICE	TOTAL
_____	Fishing for Values	$15.00	_____
_____	Visualization Cassette	$11.95	_____
		Subtotal:	_____

CA residents add 7¼% sales tax
(Santa Clara Co. residents, 8¼%): _____

Postage and handling
($2 for order up to $20; 10% of order
over $20 but less than $150;
$15 for order of $150 or more): _____

Total: _____

Resource Publications, Inc.
160 E. Virginia Street #290-BS
San Jose, CA 95112-5876
(408) 286-8505
(408) 287-8748 FAX

☐ My check or money order is enclosed.
☐ Charge my ☐ Visa ☐ MC.

Expiration Date _____

Card # _____ - _____ - _____ - _____

Signature_____

Name (print) _____

Institution_____

Street_____

City/State/zip _____